Give Me A Place
Where I May Dwell
An Ephraimite Affirmation

ALBERT JACKSON McCARN

DEDICATION

In memory of my father, Albert Jackson McCarn, Sr.
He was known as "Jack" all his life, which is "Jacob"
in another form.
Thanks to him I am a Son of Jacob (ben Yaakov).

COVER IMAGE

The picture on the cover is the proposed flag for the Ephraimite Nation. In the center is a field of black, the color of the House of Joseph established by designation of an onyx stone for Joseph in the breastplate of the High Priest (Exodus 28:15-20). On the field are twelve Stars of David (*Magen David*) representing the Twelve Tribes of Israel – not just the Ten Lost Tribes, but the portions of Judah included among them (Joseph and his companions; Ezekiel 37:15-28). The six-pointed Stars of David testify to our returning allegiance to the House of David, thus ending the rebellion of our fathers recorded in I Kings 12:16-19. The twelve stars surround a larger Star which represents the Son of David, Messiah the Prince who commands our loyalty and who will one day reunite us with our brethren of Judah. This pattern of stars recalls the two dreams of our father Joseph, who foresaw that his brothers would bow down to him (Genesis 37:5-11), and testifies to Messiah Yeshua's fulfillment of both roles as *Moshiach ben Yosef* (Messiah Son of Joseph) and *Moshiach ben David* (Messiah Son of David). The vertical white stripes speak to the purification of the saints of God through the redeeming work of Messiah. The wide stripes of royal blue remind us of the Law of our God (Numbers 15:37-41) and our calling into a priestly kingdom (Exodus 19:5-6; I Peter 2:4-10; Revelation 1:4-8, 5:9-10).

CONTENTS

ACKNOWLEDGMENTS

The Lord God of Abraham, Isaac, and Jacob inspired me to start writing and gave me the ability to do so. He gets first mention and all credit for any success of this endeavor.

The Lord put many people in my path to help me along the way. The idea to write this book sprang from discussions about the B'ney Yosef National Congress with Ephraim and Rimona Frank. They have provided immeasurable assistance in reviewing the manuscript, enriching it with their understanding of Hebrew, their years of biblical studies, their knowledge of Jewish and Israeli life, culture, and politics, and their experience in writing and publishing. Along the way they imparted a great deal of wisdom and common sense, for which I am exceedingly grateful.

Many others contributed to the birth of this project in large and small ways, often without knowing it. The list is long, but includes Batya, Hanoch, John, Katie, Ken, Neal, Nita, Pete, Sabra, Rachael, Sue, Yael, and others who have encouraged me, helped make connections and introductions, read and commented on portions of the manuscript, and opened my eyes to new ways of looking at things.

Finally, and in the chief place, I thank Charlayne, the woman who has shared my life for nearly 30 years. We have walked this road together as man and wife. I would not have come this far without her.

PREFACE

Since that uncomfortable incident in the Garden of Eden, the people of God have been expecting him to act instantaneously and immediately to fix this mess we made. If the record of the Bible is true, then God has indeed acted throughout the ages, but his timing and his manner of action have always been a surprise. Our first ancestors likely expected that after their ejection from the Garden, God would work immediately through their first children to deal with their adversary, Satan, and restore them to fellowship with him. Then they saw their oldest son murder his brother and go into exile, and hope faded. As the years accumulated they began to realize that when God said they would die on the day they ate of that forbidden fruit, he meant that they would be cut off from his life-giving presence, and that at some point in the next 1,000 years they would cease breathing. In truth, God counts the days differently than we do; one thousand years to him are as one day (II Peter 3:8; Psalm 90:4).

By that count, hardly three days have elapsed since our ancestors of the Northern Kingdom of Israel have been scattered into exile in every nation on earth. The House of Israel, led by the tribe of Ephraim, ceased being a nation when the Assyrian Empire conquered our capital city, Samaria, in 722 BCE. Since that day Israel has been defined entirely as the Jewish people, descendants of the House of Judah, the Southern Kingdom of Israel. Today Jews are the only visible remnant of the nation of Israel, but the nation is far larger than the Jewish people. God has issued prolific and astounding promises through the prophets and apostles that he would regather our people and restore us to our ancestral homeland, and that his Messiah would reunite us of Ephraim with our brethren of Judah into one kingdom, never again to be divided. This is the most extensive topic covered by the prophets, and a great hope held by the apostles in the generations after Yeshua of Nazareth completed his messianic work on a Roman execution stake. In fact, Yeshua himself spoke of this subject:

> But He answered and said, "I was sent only to the lost sheep of the house of Israel." (Matthew 15:24; see also Matthew 10:5-15)

Much confusion has surrounded this proclamation. The confusion has arisen from the misunderstanding that "Israel" and the "Jewish nation" are exactly the same. The Jewish people are most certainly the core of the Israelite nation, but they are not all of it. Yeshua and the apostles have told us that salvation is from the Jews, and that the Gospel of Messiah's kingdom goes first to the Jews and then to the rest of the world. However, from the beginning Messiah Yeshua stated his intent to begin the process of returning the rest of the tribes into the fold. In that sense, he started the fulfillment of something Hosea had prophesied many centuries earlier:

> "Come, let us return to the Lord. For He has torn *us*, but He will heal us; He has wounded *us*, but He will bandage us. He will revive us after two days; He will raise us up on the third day, that we may live before Him." (Hosea 6:1-2)

By God's reckoning, it has been two days (two thousand years) since Messiah's time. We are at the dawn of the "third day", the third millennium since Yeshua walked this earth and completed his work of redemption. We are nearing the end of the third day since our people ceased being a people. Is it time that the dry bones are to be reassembled? And if so, how is that to happen? Who will do it?

These are the questions this work addresses. Many students of prophecy have looked at these very days as the time of Messiah's return (or Messiah's coming, according to the Jewish perspective). Christian scholars have spun out their scenarios of Christ's return, but have failed to take into account that all Israel, not just the Jews, have a part in that drama. Jewish scholars have theorized as well, but their scenarios have not taken into account that the returning Lost Tribes may not be Jewish, that they may not be recognizable as tribes, and that in fact they may be classified as "Christian" by many definitions of the term. All have failed to consider the role of human beings in this great work at the conclusion of this age. Too often God's people have been waiting for him to act, not realizing that he is waiting for us to do our part. He will indeed act, but there are certain responsibilities and obligations he expects his people to meet to demonstrate their readiness for him to act. The Apostle James said as much in his letter to the Twelve Tribes scattered abroad, instructing us that "faith without works is dead" (James 2:26)

What are these works we are to do? We can take a clue from the works done over the last 150 years by our brethren of Judah. The rising tide of anti-Semitism in Europe prompted visionary Jewish men and women to take positive action on behalf of their people. Out of their vision came the Zionist Movement, the vehicle by which the hopes and dreams of Jews down through the ages finally achieved reality. Although largely secular at its inception, today the religious element of the Zionist Movement is quite prominent. The movement continues to work on behalf of the Jewish people as a distinct ethnic and religious minority among the peoples of the earth. There is some recognition in Zionism of the special nature of Jews as the "Chosen People", but not necessarily a conscious intent to fulfill God's promises to restore Judah to the Land of Israel. Nevertheless, since the late 19th century God has used the Zionist Movement, and still uses it to bring the rest of the Jewish people home.

Today he is using the Zionist Movement in a new way: to inspire the return of the rest of Israel who are not Jewish. For the last generation the Holy Spirit has been drawing people back to their Israelite heritage in many different ways. Throughout the world this phenomenon has taken the form of the Torah Awakening, a realization among Christians that the traditions and doctrines of the church in its many forms have missed something vital. Specifically, people of faith have missed their identity as Israelites, the promises of God to restore them to the Land of their fathers, and their responsibilities and obligations to return to his covenants and to the Law (Torah) which governs his covenants and their conduct within them. This movement has created a people who have come out of the church, and who are seeking where to go next.

This work is an attempt to provide direction and some answers. It has drawn inspiration directly from the work of Theodore Herzl, in many ways the founder of Zionism. In 1896 Herzl published his groundbreaking work, *Der Judenstaat (The Jewish State)*, a book which translated the theoretical postulations about solutions to the "Jewish Problem" into a plan of action. That plan became reality over the next generation, resulting in establishment of the State of Israel 50 years later.

Such is the intent of this work. Whether it will be a groundbreaking publication is yet to be determined, but its writing coincides with plans to convene the B'ney Yosef (Sons of Joseph) National Congress in 2015. This Congress has the potential to do what the First Zionist Congress did in 1897: create a sense of community and nationhood among a people who at the moment are "not a people" (I Peter 2:9-10; Deuteronomy 32:21; Hosea 1:8-11, 2:23; Romans 9:25, 10:19). From this will come a plan of action to assemble the dry bones of the House of Israel as we wait expectantly for the Spirit of God to attach the bones with sinews and put flesh on and breathe life into them. Indeed, if he is not in this work, it will come to nothing very quickly. But if it is God's timing, and if we are moving as he desires, then the world will see something it has never seen before (Ezekiel 37:10).

1

"GIVE ME A PLACE WHERE I MAY DWELL"

It is a perilous thing to start taking God at his word. He tends to change one's paradigms in most uncomfortable ways. When once we begin studying the Bible with the same amount of devotion with which we study our bank accounts, or the record of our favorite sports team, or the latest offerings from Hollywood, we find that what we have held to be true all our lives is often not quite so. Take, for example, the message of one of the world's most cherished Christmas carols, *Away in a Manger.* For the most part this pleasant song is a wonderful hymn to our Savior Yeshua haMashiach (Jesus Christ) who humbled himself to become one of us. But then we come to the last lyric:

Bless all the dear children
In Thy tender care;
And take us to heaven
To live with Thee there.

Although the Scripture says we are seated with Messiah in heavenly places (Ephesians 2:6), and that we have a heavenly calling (Hebrews 3:1-2), heaven is not our permanent home. Messiah came to earth the first time to set apart a people for his Name's sake, and is coming back with those who are in him to rule on earth for eternity. Thus *Away in a Manger* is a very nice sentiment, but not entirely accurate according to what the Bible actually says. Whatever may happen between death and resurrection, our eternal place and inheritance is not in heaven, but on earth with Messiah. That was God's promise and commission to our first ancestors:

> God created man in His own image, in the image of God He created him; male and female He created them. God blessed them; and God said to them, "Be fruitful and multiply, and fill the earth, and subdue it; and rule over the fish of the sea and over the birds of the sky and over every living thing that moves on the earth." (Genesis 1:27-28)[1]

We have also this assertion from the Psalms:

> The heavens are the heavens of the Lord, but the earth He has given to the sons of men. (Psalm 115:16)

And then we have these words from Yeshua himself:

> Blessed are the gentle ["meek"], for they shall inherit the earth. (Matthew 5:5)

Where do we get this idea that the eternal home for God's people is in heaven? Apparently from the fact that the saints of God become part of the *Kingdom of Heaven* (see Matthew 5:3, 10). But how can we become part of the Kingdom of Heaven if we do not live in heaven? *Because Heaven comes to earth to dwell with us.* That is the meaning of these words from the Apostle John:

Then I saw a new heaven and a new earth; for the first heaven and the first earth passed away, and there is no longer *any* sea. And I saw the holy city, new Jerusalem, coming down out of heaven from God, made ready as a bride adorned for her husband. And I heard a loud voice from the throne, saying, **"Behold, the tabernacle of God is among men, and He will dwell among them, and they shall be His people, and God Himself will be among them**, and He will wipe away every tear from their eyes; and there will no longer be *any* death; there will no longer be *any* mourning, or crying, or pain; the first things have passed away." (Revelation 21:1-4, emphasis added)

Let that concept soak into your consciousness for a moment. Consider how it shapes our understanding of God's eternal plan. Does it help explain why there has been so much trouble and pain on this earth for all of recorded history? I hope so. If the Holy God of all the universe is to make his home right here on this insignificant little planet, he must make it a suitable dwelling. Moreover, he must make us, the inhabitants of his new home, suitable to attend his Presence. The Scriptures explain that process in some detail, but it is not the subject of this particular writing. What I would like to address is who exactly inherits the earth, and where precisely they will live.

This is where we get to another of those long-held misconceptions. The misunderstanding in question concerns the land and people of Israel. What we know for certain is that Messiah will reign from the land of Israel, from the city of Jerusalem, both during his Millennial Kingdom (Isaiah 2:1-4; Ezekiel 43:1-9; Zechariah 14:1-21; Revelation 20:4-6) and in eternity when the New Jerusalem comes down from heaven (Revelation 21:1-27). What gets muddled in our thinking is who exactly gets to live in Israel. If we examine Scripture we will see to whom God promised the land. When we do that we learn a shocking truth: *God did not promise the land of Israel exclusively to the Jews.*

The promise concerns that particular Land on the eastern shore of the Mediterranean Sea between the River of Egypt and the River Euphrates. According to Scripture, the Lord promised it to Abraham, Isaac, and Jacob, and to their descendants forever. In other words, to the seed of Abraham through his son Isaac and grandson Jacob. The key passage is Genesis 15:

> After these things the word of the Lord came to Abram in a vision, saying, "Do not fear, Abram, I am a shield to you; your reward shall be very great." Abram said, "O Lord God, what will You give me, since I am childless, and the heir of my house is Eliezer of Damascus?" And Abram said, "Since You have given no offspring to me, one born in my house is my heir." Then behold, the word of the Lord came to him, saying, "This man will not be your heir; but one who will come forth from your own body, he shall be your heir." And He took him outside and said, "Now look toward the heavens, and count the stars, if you are able to count them." And He said to him, "So shall your descendants be." Then he believed in the Lord; and He reckoned it to him as righteousness. **And He said to him, "I am**

the Lord who brought you out of Ur of the Chaldeans, to give you this land to possess it." He said, "O Lord God, how may I know that I will possess it?" So He said to him, "Bring Me a three year old heifer, and a three year old female goat, and a three year old ram, and a turtledove, and a young pigeon." Then he brought all these to Him and cut them in two, and laid each half opposite the other; but he did not cut the birds. The birds of prey came down upon the carcasses, and Abram drove them away. Now when the sun was going down, a deep sleep fell upon Abram; and behold, terror *and* great darkness fell upon him. *God* said to Abram, "Know for certain that your descendants will be strangers in a land that is not theirs, where they will be enslaved and oppressed four hundred years. But I will also judge the nation whom they will serve, and afterward they will come out with many possessions. As for you, you shall go to your fathers in peace; you will be buried at a good old age. Then in the fourth generation they will return here, for the iniquity of the Amorite is not yet complete." It came about when the sun had set, that it was very dark, and behold, *there appeared* a smoking oven and a flaming torch which passed between these pieces. **On that day the Lord made a covenant with Abram, saying, "To your descendants I have given this land, from the river of Egypt as far as the great river, the river Euphrates: the Kenite and the Kenizzite and the Kadmonite and the Hittite and the Perizzite**

and the Rephaim and the Amorite and the Canaanite and the Girgashite and the Jebusite." (Genesis 15:1-21, emphasis added)

The Lord later confirmed that eternal covenant, promising again to give the land to Abram, and changing his name to Abraham (Genesis 17:1-15). In the next generations, God renewed the covenant with Abraham's son Isaac (Genesis 26:1-5) and grandson Jacob, whom he renamed Israel (Genesis 28:10-15, 32:22-32, 35:9-15). Still later, the Lord renewed the covenant with the entire nation of Israel after he brought them out of slavery in Egypt (Exodus19:3-6). Much later still, as judgment was coming upon the remnant of Israel for breaking that covenant, the Lord promised to renew the covenant once again. His exact words in this New, or Renewed, Covenant are:

"Behold, days are coming," declares the Lord, "when I will make a new covenant with the house of Israel and with the house of Judah, not like the covenant which I made with their fathers in the day I took them by the hand to bring them out of the land of Egypt, My covenant which they broke, although I was a husband to them," declares the Lord. "But this is the covenant which I will make with the house of Israel after those days," declares the Lord, "I will put My law within them and on their heart I will write it; and I will be their God, and they shall be My people. They will not teach again, each man his neighbor and each man his brother, saying, 'Know the Lord,' for they will all know Me, from the least of them to the greatest of them," declares the

Lord, "for I will forgive their iniquity, and their sin I will remember no more." Thus says the Lord, Who gives the sun for light by day and the fixed order of the moon and the stars for light by night, Who stirs up the sea so that its waves roar; the Lord of hosts is His name: "If this fixed order departs from before Me," declares the Lord, "Then the offspring of Israel also will cease from being a nation before Me forever." Thus says the Lord, "If the heavens above can be measured and the foundations of the earth searched out below, then I will also cast off all the offspring of Israel for all that they have done," declares the Lord. "Behold, days are coming," declares the Lord, "when the city will be rebuilt for the Lord from the Tower of Hananel to the Corner Gate. The measuring line will go out farther straight ahead to the hill Gareb; then it will turn to Goah. And the whole valley of the dead bodies and of the ashes, and all the fields as far as the brook Kidron, to the corner of the Horse Gate toward the east, shall be holy to the Lord; it will not be plucked up or overthrown anymore forever." (Jeremiah 31:31-40)

Did you notice a peculiar thing about all of those covenants? All of them apply to Abraham and his descendants, and since the time of Jacob those descendants have been called "Israel". But did you see Jews mentioned in any of these covenantal passages? That is the peculiar thing which people of faith have seldom understood, but which the Prophet Isaiah explains when he addresses the Two Houses of Israel:

> Then he shall become a sanctuary; but **to both the houses of Israel**, a stone to strike and a rock to stumble over, *and* a snare and a trap for the inhabitants of Jerusalem. (Isaiah 8:14, emphasis added)

I assure you that Jews are indeed in each of these covenants. Jews are of the seed of Abraham (Romans 9:3-5). In the Renewed Covenant they are identified as the "House of Judah". However, Jews are not the only persons in this covenant. The Lord God makes his covenants with the entire nation of Israel, not just the Jews. In fact, when he renewed the covenant with the nation of Israel at Mount Sinai, the people who would eventually become the Jews constituted only about one-fifth of the thirteen tribes numbered in the first census of the people (Numbers 2:1-3:28). Specifically, they were the royal tribes of Judah and Benjamin and the priestly tribe of Levi. When the nation of Israel split into two parts after the reign of King Solomon, those tribes became the Kingdom of Judah, so named after the ruling tribe (I Kings 12:21; II Chronicles 11:1, 13-15). The other ten tribes became known as the House of Israel, or House of Ephraim, because Ephraim, the ruling tribe, carried the name of Israel. That was the birthright inheritance passed from Jacob through his son Joseph to his grandsons Ephraim and Manasseh (Genesis 48:12-16).

Why, then, does the world suppose that Jews constitute the entire nation of Israel? One reason is because Jews are the only visible remnant of the nation of Israel still identifiable today, but the greatest reason is because few people bother to read the entire Bible. If they did they would see that the name "Jew" (in Hebrew, *Yehudi* (יהודי)) does not even appear in Scripture until the later portions of II Kings, initially in an account of events just preceding the Assyrian conquest of the Northern Kingdom (II Kings 16:6), and then after the final Babylonian conquest of the Kingdom of Judah (II Kings 25:25). Chronologically speaking, the first consistent use of the name is in the book of Jeremiah, again at the time of the Babylonian conquests, about 800 years after the death of Moses. This testimony of Scripture indicates a need to distinguish between these two parts of Israel. But who, then, are these other Israelites who are not Jews?

That answer is also clear in Scripture. Although the world has come to understand a distinction between Jew and Gentile, the Scriptural distinction is between Israel and the nations (Gentiles; *goyim* (גוים) in Hebrew). God has made eternal covenants with Israel, but he has not made any covenants with the nations. Anyone who wants to enjoy eternal life in the Presence of the Lord must be part of Israel. Scripture abounds with promises to regather and restore all of Israel – both the Jews and the Ten Tribes – under the rulership of Messiah. Ezekiel 37, Ezekiel 47:13-48:35, and Revelation 7:1-8 are prominent among these abundant references promising to restore the entire nation, tribe by tribe, into the land. That is how God intends to redeem the entire earth and the nations thereof, just as the Prophet Isaiah says:

> Now it will come about that in the last days the mountain of the house of the Lord will be established as the chief of the mountains, and will be raised above the hills; and all the nations

will stream to it. And many peoples will come and say, "Come, let us go up to the mountain of the Lord, to the house of the God of Jacob; that He may teach us concerning His ways and that we may walk in His paths." For the law [Torah] will go forth from Zion and the word of the Lord from Jerusalem. And He will judge between the nations, and will render decisions for many peoples; and they will hammer their swords into plowshares and their spears into pruning hooks. Nation will not lift up sword against nation, and never again will they learn war. (Isaiah 2:2-4; see also Micah 4:1-3)

Where are these tribes now? Many of them are Christians. Regardless what their specific ancestry, by virtue of their profession of faith in Messiah Yeshua, they are grafted back into the nation of Israel. That is the unmistakable lesson of Romans 4:13-17, 9:6-9, 11:1-36, and Ephesians 2. When Paul writes about the "fullness of the Gentiles" in Romans 11:25, he is not discussing a certain number of people who will be saved, but the multitude of people coming out of the nations and gathered into the House of Israel. That term "fullness of the Gentiles" corresponds to the Hebrew term *melo ha-goyim* (מלא הגוים). The phrase appears in Jacob's blessing of his grandsons Ephraim and Manasseh, when he says of them:

"I know, my son, I know; he [Manasseh] also will become a people and he also will be great. However, his younger brother [Ephraim] shall be greater than he, and **his descendants shall become a multitude of nations**." (Genesis 48:19, emphasis added)

The understanding from this and related Scripture is that Ephraim, the birthright tribe which bears the name of the House of Israel, has the mission of carrying the seed of Abraham into the nations (Gentiles) of the world, just as Moses prophesied regarding the destiny of Joseph:

> Of Joseph he said, "Blessed of the Lord *be* his land, with the choice things of heaven, with the dew, and from the deep lying beneath, and with the choice yield of the sun, and with the choice produce of the months. And with the best things of the ancient mountains, and with the choice things of the everlasting hills, and with the choice things of the earth and its fullness, and the favor of Him who dwelt in the bush. Let it come to the head of Joseph, and to the crown of the head of the one distinguished among his brothers. **As the firstborn of his ox, majesty is his, and his horns are the horns of the wild ox; with them he will push the peoples, all at once, *to* the ends of the earth. And those are the ten thousands of Ephraim, and those are the thousands of Manasseh.**" (Deuteronomy 33:13-17, emphasis added)

Ephraim and Manasseh are the two horns of Joseph that push the rest of the tribes to the ends of the earth, fulfilling the covenant of multiplicity promised to the Patriarchs. Yeshua has used them, and continues to do so to declare the "Good News" to their brethren by bringing his testimony of salvation and the commandments of the Lord written in his Word. In this way they fulfill the promise of God's covenant with Abraham that through him all the nations of the earth would be blessed (Genesis 22:18; Galatians 3:13-29). Then, at the end of the age, Messiah will gather again all the tribes, joining Israel/Ephraim with Judah and restoring the whole nation to the land, just as Jeremiah says:

> For thus says the Lord, "Sing aloud with gladness for Jacob, and shout among the chief of the nations; proclaim, give praise and say, 'O Lord, save Your people, the remnant of Israel.' Behold, I am bringing them from the north country, and I will gather them from the remote parts of the earth, among them the blind and the lame, the woman with child and she who is in labor with child, together; a great company, they will return here. With weeping they will come, and by supplication I will lead them; I will make them walk by streams of waters, on a straight path in which they will not stumble; **for I am a father to Israel, and Ephraim is My firstborn**." (Jeremiah 31:7-9, emphasis added)

This brings us back to the question of the moment: who shall live in the land of Israel? Obviously the nation of Israel inherits the land, but who is Israel? *Israel is those who have the testimony of Messiah and keep the commandments of God* (Deuteronomy 18:15-19; Isaiah 8:16-22; Jeremiah 23:5-8; Revelation 12:17, 14:12). It is not just the Jews, and it is not just the Christians. We are seeing the truth of this manifested before our eyes right now as Jews are awakening to the identity of Messiah and Christians are awakening to the eternal Torah of God. The time has come for the realization to dawn on us that we all have a place in the nation promised to our forefathers known as Greater Israel. The day is now here to articulate this claim. Our brethren of Judah have done very well by returning to the land and reestablishing the nation under the outstretched arm of the Lord. We of Ephraim have the obligation to help them as much as we can, not the least by continuing in prayer for Judah, and by giving of our time and resources to establish and strengthen connections with the global Jewish community and the State of Israel. In addition, we have a responsibility to learn and live by the commandments of the God of Abraham, Isaac, and Jacob, just as we have been taught by Yeshua, the one we believe to be Messiah (Matthew 5:17-19; John 14:15, 21, 15:10). But now it is time to consider our own homecoming, and therefore all of us should be ready to make considerable adjustments. Isaiah explained this to us long ago when he wrote:

> But Zion said, "The Lord has forsaken me, and my Lord has forgotten me." "Can a woman forget her nursing child, and not have compassion on the son of her womb? Surely they may forget, yet I will not forget you. See, I have inscribed you on the palms *of My hands;* your walls *are* continually before Me. Your sons shall make haste; your destroyers and those who laid you waste shall go away from you. Lift up your eyes, look around and see; all these gather together *and* come to you. *As* I live," says the Lord, "You shall surely clothe yourselves with them all as an ornament, and bind them *on you* as a bride *does.* For your waste and desolate places, and the land of your destruction, will even now be too small for the

inhabitants; and those who swallowed you up will be far away. **The children you will have, after you have lost the others, will say again in your ears, 'The place *is* too small for me; give me a place where I may dwell.'** Then you will say in your heart, 'Who has begotten these for me, since I have lost my children and am desolate, a captive, and wandering to and fro? And who has brought these up? There I was, left alone; but these, where *were* they?'" (Isaiah 49:14-21 New King James Version, emphasis added)[2]

To Zion we say: "We are your children; we are ready to return."

To the nations we have called home these many centuries we say, "Do not hinder us; the day is dawning for our return to the land of our fathers."

To our brethren of Judah we say, "Help us, that we may dwell together in peace."

It is going to be a very interesting homecoming.

---

[1] Unless otherwise indicated, all Scripture references are from the New American Standard Bible (NASB), Copyright © 1960, 1962, 1963, 1968, 1971, 1972, 1973, 1975, 1977, 1995 by The Lockman Foundation.

[2] The New King James Version®. Copyright © 1982 by Thomas Nelson.

2

RECLAIMING THE NAME OF OUR FATHERS

A Tale of Two Kingdoms

Once upon a time there was a great kingdom in a beautiful land. Not everyone in this kingdom was happy, but all were blessed. This particular kingdom was different from all the other nations and kingdoms of the world because God himself had built it. He chose the family that would be the seed of the kingdom, he preserved that family and multiplied them, and in time he brought them to the land he had designated for their dwelling place. Even though the people did not completely follow their God with perfect obedience, he still loved his kingdom enough to find a way to keep it in the blessed land. He sent judges and prophets to teach the people the right way to live, and when they refused to listen he allowed enemies to oppress them to get their attention so they would turn back to him. Time after time the people learned the lesson and returned to their God, but then another generation would grow up and wander away and have to learn the same hard lesson all over again.

Eventually the people grew tired of this cycle. They asked God to give them a king, thinking that perhaps if they were more like the nations around them they would have an easier life. God answered their request and gave them a king, but that king did not turn out to be very good, so God chose another man to rule his kingdom. That man was not perfect, but he did try to follow God with all his heart, and because of that God promised that he would always have descendants who could sit on the throne and rule the kingdom. But then a terrible thing happened. The Good King died and left the kingdom to his son, and although the new king was wise, he did not have the same heart for God as his father. In his later years the Wise King grew foolish; he decided to stop following God and to worship false gods instead. Even though God warned him many times, the king refused to listen. The king's idolatry led the people away from God and threatened the very life of the kingdom. God had to make a very hard decision and do something unpleasant just to keep the kingdom from being destroyed.

When that Foolish Wise King died, his son became the new king, but not of the whole kingdom. He was a harsh taskmaster who vexed the people, so God appointed a man to lead the people in rebellion against him. In time this leader established a separate kingdom that was continuously at war with the original kingdom. God had told this Rebel King that he would bless him and his kingdom if he would follow God's ways, but the Rebel King had ideas of his own. Not only did he lead the people away from allegiance to the Good King's descendants, he led them into rebellion against God himself. He set up a brand new religion and told the people the God they worshipped had now taken the shape of a golden calf, and he told them it was quite all right to do the things God had told them not to do. This Rebel King set a pattern that just got worse and worse. Not one of the many kings who came after him followed God. In time God had no choice but to demolish that part of the kingdom and send the people away from the land. And yet he gave them a promise: even though they were to be scattered to the four corners of the earth and mixed with every other nation and people, and even though they would forget who they were, God would one day bring them back to the land. God would change their hearts while they were in exile so that they would be able to follow him. When the time was right they would remember who they were and what they had done to earn God's anger, and then they would return to God in repentance. And once that happened, God would bring them back to the kingdom.

But what of the other part of the kingdom, the part that did not rebel against the Good King's grandson? That kingdom eventually fell away from God as well. Long after the rebellious kingdom was sent into exile, God had to destroy this other kingdom and send those people away also. Yet they had a different destiny. Some of them came back to the land after a time, and they tried very hard to be faithful to God. It was through them that God brought a great Man, a descendant of that Good King, who would pay with his very own life to satisfy the sentence of death that the rebellion of both kingdoms had incurred. Then this One returned to life and sent his followers out into the world to gather the scattered people back into the kingdom. Yet his very own people did not know who he was. Although they clung to the words God had written in his Book, they rejected the living Word of God, and for that they incurred another sentence of exile into the nations. And so it was that both parts of God's kingdom were dispersed into the entire earth: the first rebellious ones who had rejected the Written Word of God, but who began to embrace the Living Word; and the second rebellious ones who held fast to the Written Word, but rejected the Living Word.

For many, many years the two parts of the kingdom did not want to have anything to do with one another. They fought bitterly and regarded one another with contempt. The descendants of the first rebellious kingdom grew in numbers, power, and wealth, but they lost their identity as a people. They also grew in jealousy toward their brethren of the second rebellious kingdom, who diminished in numbers, but retained their identity as a people. Little did these first rebellious ones know that in harassing their brethren they were killing their own flesh and blood, and in a sense eating their own children. The two antagonistic brethren could not see that they had sprung from the same family, or that the same instructions from the same God established the standards for the way they lived and the hopes they held for the future. Each one had a portion of the full truth, but none could see the whole picture. Each one refused to consider that they might be missing some of the truth, and that what they were missing was what the other part of the kingdom had.

And so it continues to this day. The kingdom God made is called Israel. The rulers of Israel were

David, the Good King known as the man after God's own heart, Solomon, the Foolish Wise King, Rehoboam, the Harsh King, and Jeroboam, the Rebel King. After David's death, the wise but idolatrous Solomon incurred God's judgment, which took the form of Jeroboam's rebellion against Rehoboam. When Jeroboam became ruler of the Northern Kingdom of Israel, Rehoboam was left with only a small part of the kingdom built around his own tribe of Judah. And then came more error, more idolatry, more rebellion, until God sentenced both kingdoms to exile, but with the added measure of amnesia for the Northern Kingdom. In time Messiah Yeshua (Jesus Christ) came to and through Judah, but his own people, the Jews, rejected him. His message of redemption and salvation went out nonetheless to all the earth, and millions embraced it. Their hearts had been prepared by a vague remembrance of the true God that remained in the consciousness of Israelite exiles, and thus the Christian church in its various manifestations grew. Yet through the ages Christians and Jews have continued to distrust and shun one another, not understanding that each has something the other needs, and that God's promise to restore his kingdom depends on them coming together as one people again.

Could this restoration ever happen? Yes. It is happening even now. Jews, the people of Judah, have returned to the land and reestablished a portion of the nation of Israel. There is an awakening among Jews worldwide to the fact that Yeshua of Nazareth is very Jewish, and that his followers in Christianity need to be acquainted with that fact and with the Hebraic nature of their faith. Some Jews are open to the possibility that Yeshua is at least a manifestation of the promised Messiah, and some have even accepted his Messianic claims. Perhaps more importantly, there is a growing awareness of the fact that a Jew who accepts Yeshua as Messiah does not lose his or her "Jewishness". These are good things, but they are only the beginning.

The Messianic Movement among Jews has served as a catalyst for an awakening among Christians that they have missed something in their faith. Specifically, they have missed the commandments of God given through the Torah written by Moses, as well as the Hebraic understanding of the entire Word of God. These Christians are not becoming Jews, and they are not rejecting Messiah Yeshua, but rather are seeing Yeshua in his Hebraic context and following his example in keeping the Shabbat (Sabbath), celebrating the Feasts of the Lord (commonly called the "Jewish Feasts"), refusing to eat pork and other unclean meats, and turning from the paganized forms of worship that have crept into Christian practices over the centuries. Many Christians who are not yet ready to become Torah-observant are at least open to learning about the "Jewish roots" of their faith, and even though Messianic or Hebrew Roots believers are not yet fully accepted in all Christian circles, there is at least a growing tolerance of them among many Christians who sense that God is doing something different in our day.

These, too, are good things, but they also are only the beginning. They herald something much, much bigger. These are signs of the coming restoration of all Israel.

Looking for the Lost Tribes

It is relatively easy to identify that part of Israel known as Judah. They are the Jews. God has proved his faithfulness and his ability to come through on his promises by preserving the Jews as a people and by bringing them back to the Land of Israel. The process of Judah's restoration is not yet complete; there are almost as many recognized Jews living outside the State of Israel than in it, and still more who are rediscovering and embracing their Jewish ancestry after centuries of hiding it. The very existence of the State of Israel is an unmistakable sign of God's certain and soon completion of his promise to restore the entire nation. That means not just the Jews, but also the exiles of the Northern Kingdom, known by various names including Israel, Samaria, B'ney Yosef (Sons of Joseph), and Ephraim. The greater part of Ephraim's population were the Ten Tribes of Ephraim, Manasseh, Reuben, Simeon, Dan, Naphtali, Gad, Asher, Issachar, and Zebulun. In Israel today there remains a small group of about 800 Samaritans, descendants of the Ten Tribes who mixed with other nations brought in by the Assyrians who conquered Israel in the 8th century BCE. The name "B'ney Yosef" refers to the tribes of Ephraim and Manasseh, the sons of Joseph who were adopted by their grandfather Jacob and given a place among their eleven uncles as fathers of tribes in Israel. Collectively all of these Ten Tribes could also be called "Ephraim" because the kings who rebelled against the House of David and split from Judah were of the tribe of Ephraim. Moreover, when Jacob adopted his grandsons, he passed on to Ephraim the birthright blessing, which meant that Ephraim would

carry Jacob's new name of Israel and, with his uncle
Judah, would produce the rulers of the entire nation.[1]
Thus, when the Ten Tribes rebelled, they took the
name of Israel because the chief tribe, Ephraim,
carried the family name (Genesis 48:14-16). At times
Ephraim is used generically to describe the prophetic
destiny of the "Lost Tribes".

As the Scripture explains, Joseph's birthright
blessing entailed a double portion and a higher status
than his brothers. That is why both of Joseph's sons
became fathers of tribes. Judah, however, was to be
the father of the kings of all Israel, and through him
would come Messiah, the Son of David. After the
division of the kingdom, the southern portion took
the name Judah and continued to be ruled by the
Davidic Dynasty. Those who remained loyal to the
House of David were the tribe of Benjamin and the
priestly tribe of Levi. During the centuries of ancient
Israel's time in the land, including the two hundred
years in which Israel and Judah existed as hostile
sovereign kingdoms, there was much interaction and
mixing among the tribes. When the exile occurred,
the House of Ephraim and the House of Judah each
contained significant remnants of one another in their
scattered populations. Thus the world's Jewish
population contains elements of all the tribes, as well
as bloodlines of non-Israelite peoples who have
mixed with or married into the Jewish community.
And that is precisely the advantage Judah has over
Ephraim: *there actually exists an identifiable Jewish
community that could be transformed into a nation through the
Zionist Movement.*

Ephraim has not enjoyed the advantage of Judah.
There are a few thousand people living in India who

identify themselves as "Bnei Ephraim" and "Bnei Menashe", descendants of Joseph's sons Ephraim and Manasseh, but other than that there is at the time of this writing no identifiable people known as Ephraimites, or B'ney Yosef. Where are these tribes and how can they be identified? Those are questions many scholars have sought to answer. The paths of the exiles may have faded over the centuries, but they are not impossible to follow. It is not the purpose of this work to provide an exhaustive review of Lost Tribes scholarship, but rather to accept its validity and build on it. The evidence is significant, starting with the biblical records:

> In the ninth year of Hoshea, the king of Assyria captured Samaria and carried Israel away into exile to Assyria, and settled them in Halah and Habor, *on* the river of Gozan, and in the cities of the Medes. (II Kings 17:6; see also II Kings 18:11 and I Chronicles 5:26)

The first place to look is in the region formerly known as Assyria, and in the ancient homeland of the people known as the Medes. Those areas are now known as northern Iraq, southeastern Turkey, and northwestern Iran. Is there a people living in those regions with a claim of descent from the Medes, and thus at least partially from Israel? Yes. They are called the Kurds[2]. Yet they are not the only ones. The Yusufzai ("Sons of Joseph") among the Pashtun peoples of Afghanistan and Pakistan are also at least partially descended from the tribes of Ephraim and Manasseh.[3] Still others may be found among the Bnei Menashe, a people of eastern India who have maintained their identity as descendants of the tribe of Manasseh, and who are even now returning to

Israel as the first among the Lost Tribes with official rabbinical recognition.[4]   Research into linguistic, anthropological, genetic (DNA), historical, and religious evidence has shown migration patterns of the Ephraimite Tribes to the north, east, west, and south, including Northern and Western Europe and the British Isles.[5]   During the age of Europe's empires, the Ephraimite elements of the Spanish, British, French, German, Belgian, and Italian nations spread throughout the colonies of the Americas, Africa, Australia, Asia, New Zealand, and the Pacific Islands. It may safely be concluded, therefore, that in the 2,700 years of Ephraim's exile, the physical seed of Israel's tribes has spread to every single nation and people group on earth. Many of these peoples have become Christians, which seems to fit with God's promise through the Prophet Ezekiel:

> Therefore say, "Thus says the Lord God, 'Though I had removed them far away among the nations and though I had scattered them among the countries, yet I was a sanctuary for them a little while in the countries where they had gone.'" (Ezekiel 11:16)

In other words, these scattered peoples would forget their identity, but they would not entirely forget their God. Thus, when the message of redemption through Messiah Yeshua arrived through missionaries, these Ephraimites were primed to receive it. Yet the watered-down, paganized version of the Gospel of the Kingdom which has prevailed in Christianity for the last 1,700 years did not impart the full message that these peoples were actually Israelites grafted back into the kingdom of Israel by the work of Yeshua (a truth the Apostle Paul explains in

Romans 11). That message had to wait until our day before the world was ready for it. And now it appears that the next portion of Ezekiel's prophecy is about to be fulfilled:

> Therefore say, "Thus says the Lord God, 'I will gather you from the peoples and assemble you out of the countries among which you have been scattered, and I will give you the land of Israel.'" (Ezekiel 11:17)

Yet if God is to gather his people of Ephraim, they should be made ready for the gathering. Something is still missing in that Ephraim is still not readily identifiable among the nations. What is lacking is a national consciousness, a sense of Ephraim as a people group living in exile among the nations. Such an awakening began among the Jews of Europe about 150 years ago. The awakening gained momentum in 1882 with the First *Aliyah*, when groups of Jews from Europe and from Yemen embarked separately and simultaneously on their return to the Land of Israel. Soon thereafter the Jews of Europe led the way in building a national consciousness through a movement known as Zionism. The Zionist Movement transformed Judah from an assortment of communities scattered among the nations to a nation-in-exile actively seeking restoration to its ancient homeland. That is precisely what should happen to Ephraim. To put it biblically, Ephraimites must become what the Hebrew language calls an *Am*, a people, just as the Prophet Hosea foretold:

> Yet the number of the sons of Israel will be like the sand of the sea, which cannot be measured or numbered; and in the place where it is said to them, "You are not My people [*lo-ammi*]," it

will be said to them, "*You are* the sons of the living God." (Hosea 1:10)

Imagining Ephraim: Bringing the Vision into Being

What is Ephraim lacking? Quite simply it is the will to envision or "imagine" ourselves as Ephraim. In this we may draw help from Dr. Benedict Anderson and his groundbreaking work, *Imagined Communities: Reflections on the Origin and Spread of Nationalism*. Anderson writes:

> In an anthropological spirit, then, I propose the following definition of the nation: it is an imagined political community – and imagined as both inherently limited and sovereign. It is *imagined* because the members of even the smallest nation will never know most of their fellow-members, meet them, or even hear of them, yet in the minds of each lives the image of their communion.[6]

We infer from this definition that a nation is a nation because its citizens say so. There is, of course, some kind of bond that unites the people into this community they imagine. Sometimes it is a common racial or ethnic heritage, such as that which defines the Native American nations like the Navajo, Lakota, Nez Percé, and Cherokee. Or the bond may be a common language and culture, such as that of the German, Italian, and Polish nations. The bond may also be political, such as that which defined the United Kingdom of Great Britain in the union of England, Scotland, Wales, and Northern Ireland, or which motivated the establishment of the United States of America. In such a nation as the United

States, racial, ethnic, linguistic, cultural, and religious factors contribute aspects of a diverse national character, but are secondary to the political reality of the nation which establishes its existence in the minds of its citizens. As long as the citizens believe in the reality of the nation, the nation exists and can take action in the international community.

There is no single criterion or set of criteria that is required to build a nation. If the people of the would-be nation will it to be so, then it is so. It remains to be seen whether their will can be translated into concrete facts that the existing community of nations can accept. For example, my ancestors envisioned a community in the southern portion of the United States which they called the Confederate States of America. It was a nation in every sense of the word, having a political organization, a government, an army and navy, a functioning economy, diplomatic relations with other nations, and a common language and culture that united people of different ethnic, racial, and religious backgrounds. The fact that certain of the Confederacy's inhabitants were at a decided disadvantage and denied the full status of citizenship because of the color of their skin does not alter the fact that the nation did exist for a time. However, its establishment as a rival government within the territory of the United States brought about a bitter civil war which the Confederacy did not survive. Yet even though its political existence ceased, the dream of the Confederacy remained part of the consciousness of many white Southerners more than a century later.

Interestingly, while most of my Southern ancestors were imagining themselves into the Confederacy, one chose a different path. In the years before the American Civil War this man had moved to Alabama from the state of New York. As a "Yankee", his sentiments remained with the United States, not with his Southern neighbors and kin, and when Alabama joined the Confederacy, he imagined himself still part of the Union. For that reason he took up arms in defense of his beloved Union, and before the war was over he had faced his own stepson in battle at the city of Atlanta. Thus the Civil War for my family was quite literally a war of brother against brother and father against son. In this is a powerful lesson: allegiance to an imagined national community often surpasses other ties, even those of kith and kin.

The point for our purposes is that the Ephraimite nation, just like every other nation, may be imagined or envisioned into existence. We have sufficient justification to do so. The racial and ethnic component is there. That, indeed, is key to our national definition: we, like the Jews, are the seed of Abraham. Can we say so with certainty? Yes. Consider an example from the American Indian nations. I know a wise Indian teacher from a certain tribe now settled in Oklahoma. He says that he often encounters people who boast of their Native American ancestry by saying, "I'm part Indian". He replies with the question, "Which part?" He argues that it matters not whether a person is "full blood" Cherokee or Muscogee or Seminole. The fact that a person has at least one ancestor of a native tribe or tribes is enough to affirm kinship. As he says, "blood is blood".

By that reasoning, I may claim descent from ancestors who came to North America from Scotland, Ireland, and England. That much is certain based on genealogical research going back over three hundred years. But what of the previous thousand years? The history of the British Isles between the first century BCE and the tenth century CE is one of continuous migration and conflict. The native Celtic, Irish, and Pictish populations of the islands first faced wars of conquest and occupation by the Roman Empire, and after Rome's withdrawal steadily lost ground to an influx of Anglo-Saxon tribes. Just as the imagined community of Saxon England was becoming an established fact, Norse raiders from the Viking lands of Scandinavia contested Saxon rule and from time to time controlled portions of England, Scotland, and Ireland. By the time of the Norman Conquest in 1066, when a French strain was superimposed on the English ruling class, the populations of the islands were already a nearly indecipherable mix. My ancestry, therefore, includes the strains from the various upheavals of that millennium. And before that? All we can do is look at the ancient migration patterns. The Celts, Saxons, Norse, Franks, and others invaded Europe from the steppes of Central Asia in the declining years of the Roman Empire. At that time they were called Goths and Vandals. Before that they were known as Cimmerians, Scythians, and Parthians. And before that they were known as Israelites, exiled by the Assyrian Empire from their Promised Land and doomed to wander the earth in search of a home.

Ethnicity, or physical descent, does therefore comprise one of the identifying features of our

Ephraimite community. In time that reality will come more into focus. However, it is not the only distinguishing characteristic. What is now awakening Ephramites to their identity is an understanding of their spiritual heritage. That is why many Ephraimites are found in, or have come out of, the various Christian churches. They have accepted that Yeshua of Nazareth is God's Messiah, and by their faith in him have stepped into a new identity. Thus the second identifying characteristic of an Ephraimite is allegiance to Yeshua the Son of David.

The next distinguishing characteristic derives from something Moses foretold on the eve of Israel's conquest of the Promised Land:

> So it shall be when all of these things have come upon you, the blessing and the curse which I have set before you, and you call *them* to mind in all nations where the Lord your God has banished you, and you return to the Lord your God and obey Him with all your heart and soul according to all that I command you today, you and your sons, then the Lord your God will restore you from captivity, and have compassion on you, and will gather you again from all the peoples where the Lord your God has scattered you. If your outcasts are at the ends of the earth, from there the Lord your God will gather you, and from there He will bring you back. The Lord your God will bring you into the land which your fathers possessed, and you shall possess it; and He will prosper you and multiply you more than your fathers. (Deuteronomy 30:1-6)

This prophecy is at the heart of the "Torah Awakening" we are witnessing even now. Christians who are returning to their Hebrew Roots are doing so with the growing understanding that our ancestors have not followed the commandments of the Lord. We have been taught that Jesus Christ died on the cross to save the world from sin and to do away with the Law, or Torah, of God. That doctrine contradicts the clear teaching of Yeshua that he had come not to abolish the Law and the Prophets, but to live out and explain their full meaning (see Matthew 5:17-19). Hebrew Roots believers are beginning to recognize that by negating Torah the church in its various forms has perpetuated the errors of our Israelite ancestors who worshipped the Lord God in ways of their own devising, not in the ways he specified. Our religious practices, however well intentioned, have in many cases offended God. But even this was prophesied:

"As for you, O house of Israel," thus says the Lord God, "Go, serve everyone his idols; but later you will surely listen to Me, and My holy name you will profane no longer with your gifts and with your idols. For on My holy mountain, on the high mountain of Israel," declares the Lord God, "there the whole house of Israel, all of them, will serve Me in the land; there I will accept them and there I will seek your contributions and the choicest of your gifts, with all your holy things. As a soothing aroma I will accept you when I bring you out from the peoples and gather you from the lands where you are scattered; and I will prove Myself holy among you in the sight of the nations. And you will know that I am the Lord, when I bring you into the land of Israel, into the land which I swore to give to your forefathers. There you will remember your ways and all your deeds with which you have defiled yourselves; and you will loathe yourselves in your own sight for all the evil things that you have done. Then you will know that I am the Lord when I have dealt with you for My name's sake, not according to your evil ways or according to your corrupt deeds, O house of Israel," declares the Lord God. (Ezekiel 20:39-44)

This is what is happening today as Hebrew Roots believers come to the realization that we have perpetuated the very idolatry which resulted in the exile of our Ephraimite ancestors. We have exchanged the Lord's Sabbath, his Feast Days, his commandments on what to put into our bodies, and his regulations for structuring society and replaced them with traditions and doctrines that seem right to a man, but the end thereof is death. This is indeed the day when the words of Jeremiah are coming to fulfillment:

O Lord, my strength and my stronghold, and my refuge in the day of distress, to You the nations will come from the ends of the earth and say, "Our fathers have inherited nothing but falsehood, futility and things of no profit." (Jeremiah 16:19)

Thus the third component of Ephraimite identity is an adherence to God's Torah. This does not mean perfect obedience to it, but rather a heart that is open to the Holy Spirit's instruction into the Law of God and a willingness to make changes in our lives as he highlights areas that need attention. This is the very process that the Apostle James explained in the Jerusalem Council of Acts 15. There was debate about what to require of those who were coming to faith in Yeshua from among the nations ("Gentiles"). Some among the Jewish believers demanded immediate circumcision and immersion in Torah for these converts. The conclusion James reached was that it would be unreasonable to expect these people who were coming out of a pagan lifestyle to become like Jews, and certainly unreasonable to expect them to follow Jewish traditions which were not part of the Torah. A Torah-observant lifestyle such as Yeshua modeled was the goal, but these new believers needed help in going through a process of maturity to grow into that lifestyle. Therefore James recommended that the immediate obligation for new believers was that they demonstrate their departure from paganism by adhering to four specific requirements, and once that was done they would be ready to be discipled into God's standards of conduct as given in the books of Moses (Torah). That is the background of James' remarks in Acts 15:

> Therefore it is my judgment that we do not trouble those who are turning to God from among the Gentiles, but that we write to them that they abstain from things contaminated by idols and from fornication and from what is strangled and from blood. For Moses from ancient generations has in every city those who preach him, since he is read in the synagogues every Sabbath. (Acts 15:19-21)

We have, therefore, three distinct criteria as the basis of Ephraimite identity: Israelite ancestry, however tenuous; allegiance to Yeshua of Nazareth as

Messiah; and Torah observance, or at least the goal of Torah observance. These criteria are exclusive. Not all who are physical descendants of the Ten Tribes could be considered Ephraimites. The Kurds and the Yusufzai, for example, are for the most part Muslim, and therefore do not acknowledge the Messiahship of Yeshua. Thus while they may be considered our kin, they are not yet part of the nation. Likewise most Christians are not part of the nation, for though they may have the physical descent, and though they profess faith in Yeshua, they do not acknowledge the Torah as God's standard for their lives. Consequently, although we desire to have fellowship as much as possible with our Christian brethren, and live in peace with our Muslim kin, we would not expect them to be identified with the Ephraimite nation.

Then there are our brethren of the House of Judah. We share kinship as Israelites, and at least among observant Jews there is a shared regard for Torah, but we differ on the identity of Yeshua. Can we have fellowship with Jews? Yes; we can and we must. Judah is now in the Land, and we require the help of the State of Israel in establishing our part of the nation. The destiny of Judah has been different from that of Ephraim. Our histories and cultures have intersected, often tragically, and we are as different as two brothers of the same father can be. The tension between us is considerable, but as brothers we should resolve to live and work together. Our faith ultimately is in our Father God, Who has promised this through Isaiah:

> Then it will happen on that day that the Lord
> will again recover the second time with His

hand the remnant of His people, who will remain, from Assyria, Egypt, Pathros, Cush, Elam, Shinar, Hamath, and from the islands of the sea. And He will lift up a standard for the nations and assemble the banished ones of Israel, and will gather the dispersed of Judah from the four corners of the earth. Then the jealousy of Ephraim will depart, and those who harass Judah will be cut off; Ephraim will not be jealous of Judah, and Judah will not harass Ephraim. (Isaiah 11:11-13)

But what of those who are not physical descendants of Ephraim, but do profess faith in Yeshua and try to keep Torah? Are they part of Ephraim? Possibly; it depends on where they pin their identity. God has always opened the way to join with the family of Abraham, Isaac, and Jacob, but doing so requires leaving one's previous identity. The examples of Rahab the Canaanite, Ruth the Moabite, Uriah the Hittite, and Obadiah the Edomite instruct our understanding, particularly the words of Ruth:

> But Ruth said, "Do not urge me to leave you *or* turn back from following you; for where you go, I will go, and where you lodge, I will lodge. Your people *shall be* my people, and your God, my God. Where you die, I will die, and there I will be buried. Thus may the Lord do to me, and worse, if *anything but* death parts you and me." (Ruth 1:16-17)

With that declaration *Ruth ceased being a Moabite and became an Israelite.* Her subsequent actions confirmed her decision as she proved faithful not only to her mother-in-law Naomi, but to the God of Israel and his ways. So also should be the case of those who are

41

not physical descendants of Israel, but who desire to leave their previous identity and become identified with the people and nation of God.

And is that not the case for us all? To this day we have lived as Afghans, Americans, Arabs, Argentinians, Australians, Burmese, Congolese, Cubans, Dutch, Ethiopians, French, Indians, Iranians, Japanese, Kenyans, Koreans, Kurds, Mexicans, Nigerians, Russians, South Africans, and other nationalities where our scattered people have sojourned these many centuries. Our first step is to lay down our comfortable national identity and acknowledge our Ephraimite heritage in the Commonwealth of Israel. Let me be the first to do so.

Let all the world know henceforth that I am an Israelite, of the House of Joseph, of the Tribe of Ephraim. Who will join me and other committed Israelites in reconstituting our nation of the House of Joseph?

---

[1] The biblical account of Jacob's adoption of Joseph's sons is in Genesis 48, and reiterated in Jeremiah 31:8-9, the same chapter in which God promises the New (or Renewed) Covenant. The co-rulership of Joseph (through his son Ephraim) and Judah is in Jacob's prophecies over his sons in Genesis 49, and is reiterated in I Chronicles 5:1-2.

[2] M.R. Izady, "Are Kurds Descended from the Medes?," *Kurdish Life*, No. 10 (1994), http://www.kurdistanica.com/?q=node/32 (accessed January 31, 2015); Kendal Nezan, "A Brief Survey of the History of the Kurds," Fondation Institut Kurde de Paris, http://www.institutkurde.org/en/institute/who_are_the_kurds. php (accessed January 31, 2015); Mehrdad R. Izady, "Judaism", *The Kurds, A Concise Handbook*, (Harvard: 1992), http://www.kurdistanica.com/?q=node/105 (accessed January 31, 2015).

[3] Rory McCarthy, "Pashtun clue to lost tribes of Israel," *The Guardian* (January 16, 2010), http://www.theguardian.com/world/2010/jan/17/israel-lost-tribes-pashtun (accessed January 31, 2015); _____, "The Ten Lost Tribes: Afghanistan," *Moshiach Online*, http://www.moshiach.com/tribes/afghanistan.html (accessed January 31, 2015).

[4] *Bnei Menashe: Lost Tribe Coming Home*, http://www.bneimenashe.com/ (accessed January 31, 2015).

[5] The mystery of the Ten Lost Tribes is a subject that has remained on the fringes of "respectable" scholarship. Serious, credentialed scholars have done creditable research in archaeology, linguistics, anthropology, genetics, history, and other disciplines in an effort to trace the Ten Tribes through history and identify their descendants today. This research has turned up a consistent body of evidence indicating the various places to which the descendants of Israel and of Judah migrated after the ancient conquests by Assyria and Babylon. Those who would be interested in investigating and judging these things could start by reviewing the work of Yair Davidiy, Steven M. Collins, and Drs. Alex and Georgina Perdomo. Yair Davidiy, *Brit-Am, Movement of the Ten Tribes of Israel*, http://britam.org/ (accessed January 31, 2015); Yair Davidiy, *Hebrew Nations: A Britam Website*, http://hebrewnations.com/ (accessed January 31, 2015); Steven M. Collins, *History of the Ten Tribes of Israel*, http://stevenmcollins.com/homepage.php (accessed January 31, 2015); Alex and Georgina Perdomo, *Etz Yosef Project*, http://etzyoseph.org/ (accessed January 31, 2015).

[6] Benedict Anderson, *Imagined Communities: Reflections on the Origin and Spread of Nationalism*, (London & New York: Verso, 2006), 6.

3

TURNING FROM THE SIN OF OUR FATHERS

A Matter of Identity

Now that we know who we are, let us consider who we are not. *We are not Jews.*

Israel's Law of Return specifies the requirements of Jewish identity for those who wish to make *Aliyah* and become Israeli citizens. We do not meet those requirements. Our practices may look Jewish, and we may affiliate with Messianic Jewish congregations, but we are not and have no desire to be Jews. Conversion to Judaism is not our goal. We owe a great debt to the Jews who have persevered over the millennia in keeping the Oracles of God as delivered through Moses and the prophets. Thanks to them we know we have missed something vital in our relationship to our God, and thanks to them we are now finding our way back to him through the Torah Awakening. However, we do not want to *become* our Jewish brethren; we want to *join with* them and take our rightful place as fellow citizens of the Commonwealth of Israel.

There is another important misidentification we should clarify: *We are not Christians.*

Many of us come from Christian backgrounds, and we are very grateful for our Christian heritage. Thanks to this upbringing we have learned to appreciate the Bible as the Word of God, and have embraced Yeshua of Nazareth as Messiah. However, we can no longer accept or identify with the practices of Christianity which are rooted in the idolatrous pagan ways of our distant ancestors. Nor can we continue to be identified with doctrines that deny the applicability of God's Torah to all of his people, and that perpetuate the manmade division between Israel and the Church. This human invention defines Israel (often called "physical" or "natural" Israel) as only the Jewish people, the nation that "rejected Messiah" and is "stuck in the past" under the "bondage" of the Law (Torah). By this definition, the Church (often called "spiritual Israel" or "the Israel of God") is an entity which, according to its perceptions of itself, has progressed beyond Judaism into a new system established by Jesus Christ which has no relation to Torah. This deep-seated attitude produces a concept of Israelite identity so highly spiritualized as to be meaningless. At its extreme, it consigns Jews to eternal destruction and usurps their place in God's kingdom.

If we are not Jews, however much we may act, talk, and look like Jews, and if we are not Christians, however much we may think and talk like Christians, what are we? That should be clear by now:

We are non-Jewish Israelites of the House of Ephraim.

With this declaration we assert our full citizenship in the Commonwealth of Israel. We are the descendants of Abraham, Isaac, Jacob, and Jacob's sons. We do not want to replace our brethren of Judah, but neither do we want to be limited by an exclusive definition of Israel which says the nation consists only of Jews. There are blessings promised by God to us, and we join with Judah in claiming our share of those blessings. In that sense we echo the statement of our fathers long ago, after King David crushed the rebellion of his son Absalom:

> But the men of Israel answered the men of Judah and said, "We have ten parts in the king, therefore we also have more *claim* on David than you. Why then did you treat us with contempt? Was it not our advice first to bring back our king?" (II Samuel 19:43)

Our claim is that Yeshua, the Son of David, is the one to restore David's kingdom, and thus there is a prophetic element in this passage. Let us expand on this in national terms: we are ten tribes, and we have ten parts in the nation of Israel. We do not deny Judah's parts in the nation, but we claim our legitimate share.

The secular mind will not understand or appreciate the religious or spiritual aspects of our claim. Nevertheless we articulate them because without the spiritual foundation we cannot establish our identity. This book will cover the practical aspects of nation building in later chapters, but those aspects are meaningless without the spiritual underpinning.

What we are doing is different from anything done before, with the possible exception of Judah's return to the Land after the Babylonian Captivity. Two modern developments come close: the migration of Christian reformers to the New World; and the return of the Jews to the Land of Israel. Yet these do not capture the full essence of the Ephraimite Movement. The Reformation gave birth to many Christian sects, including Puritans, Separatists, Huguenots, Moravians, and Quakers. They sought a place where they could live in peace and worship God according to their understanding of the Bible, but for the most part they did not acknowledge themselves as Israelites, nor did they seek a place in the Land of Israel. In fact, they continued the pattern of migration away from the Land as they found homes in the Americas. The Zionist Movement reversed the move away from the Land by bringing Jews back just as God had promised, but it was founded largely on secular principles. The great Zionist leaders acknowledged their spiritual heritage as Jews, but their motivation was pragmatic: Jews needed a refuge from the persecution suffered in every nation where they lived, and the logical place for that refuge was their ancestral homeland on the eastern shore of the Mediterranean Sea.

The Ephraimite Movement combines elements of these two modern migrations in a unique way. For the first time in nearly three millennia, a people are arising who seek to return to their ancient ancestral homeland on the eastern shore of the Mediterranean in response to the call of their God. Like our Christian predecessors, we seek a place of refuge where we may live in peace according to our understanding of the Bible, and like our Zionist predecessors, we do so because we are Israelites and there is no other place for us. Unlike both of them, we want to carry this return through to its ultimate conclusion by building a nation based on the standards of conduct which God gave to our ancestors in his Torah and which Yeshua modeled and taught. For that reason, our nation cannot be a secular nation. *And for that reason it is necessary to acknowledge the sins of our fathers.*

Carrying Repentance to its Logical Conclusion

In recent years there has been a movement of repentance in the church worldwide. Usually this movement defines repentance as turning from blatantly immoral activities and attitudes such as human trafficking, abortion, homosexuality, and other forms of sexual immorality.[1] There is even recognition, at least in some American Evangelical circles, that emphasis on government as the means of solving national problems is itself a form of idolatry. There is an attempt to find the right balance between pious withdrawal from the political process and establishment of a Christian theocracy. That is commendable, but it is not enough. There is little recognition of the fact that modern Christianity in all its forms still practices things that displease God.

Repentance has always been an important expression of Christianity. Five hundred years ago, recognition of errors in the Roman Catholic Church sparked the Reformation which birthed the various Protestant traditions. The Reformers understood that the Catholic doctrines and practices they had followed all their lives departed significantly from the testimony of Scripture, and they took action to correct those errors. Many of the Catholic practices received institutionalization, sanction, and force of law during the reign of Emperor Constantine the Great of Rome (306-337 CE). When Constantine adopted Christianity as the official religion of Rome, he took counsel from the leading clergy of the day to standardize the religion in ways that would make it a unifying element for the empire and strengthen his hold over it. With Constantine's imperial sanction, the Church of Rome instructed God's people:

(1) That it was acceptable to worship the Lord God as an image of a man, even a man on a cross, in violation of God's commandments not to worship any image;

(2) To bring their sacrifices in the form of offerings to the new temples to the Lord built in every city rather than to Jerusalem, the place God had chosen;

(3) To celebrate new feast days to the Lord (Sunday, Christmas, Easter) instead of the ones God had specified;

(4) To follow the teachings of priests who were not of Levi, the tribe the Lord had chosen as priests.

Have we departed from the ways of Constantine? Certainly not. While we may dispute the questions of sacrifices in a Temple yet destroyed and of a priesthood yet scattered throughout the nations, we cannot deny that we have engaged in idolatry. Do not the images of saints, of Mary the Mother of God, and of Jesus himself adorn the churches of Christendom? And even the image of his empty cross has become an idol, for often we attach meaning and power to that form rather than to the Spirit Who testifies to the victory won on it.

Reformers have tinkered with the Christian religious system for nearly 1,700 years, but until now have not begun to address the deepest errors within it. Those errors go back much further in time than the advent of Christianity. Their origins lie in the sins of our ancient Israelite ancestors.

Remembering the Sins of Jeroboam

Our identity as Ephraimites means that we lay claim not only to the blessings of Abraham our father, but to the responsibilities of living in a covenant relationship with the God of Abraham, Isaac, and Jacob. If we are to reclaim our ancient heritage, we need to acknowledge the fact that our ancestors did not do very well in living up to their part of this covenant relationship. That, in fact, was why the Lord God exiled our ancestors from the Land (see II Kings 17). We are counting on the Lord to come through on his promises to gather us back from the nations and restore us to the Land, but that promise entails responsibility on our part. As Moses said:

> So it shall be when all of these things have come upon you, the blessing and the curse which I have set before you, and you call *them* to mind in all nations where the Lord your God has banished you, and you return to the Lord your God and obey Him with all your heart and soul according to all that I command you today, you and your sons, then the Lord your God will restore you from captivity, and have compassion on you, and will gather you again from all the peoples where the Lord your God has scattered you. (Deuteronomy 30:1-3)

Yeshua echoed this in his parable of the Prodigal Son (Luke 15:11-32). The prodigal had taken his share of the inheritance, left his father's house, and moved to a foreign country. There he wasted his wealth in all manner of frivolous activities. Eventually he was reduced to poverty and forced to take a job feeding pigs. In other words, he had engaged in willful disobedience, resulting in his loss of status, blessing, and identity, and had become entwined with the abominable things of the world (represented by the pigs). It was not until the prodigal recognized his situation and made a conscious decision to return to his father that things changed for the better. The father could not run after him and bring him back until he decided first that he wanted to come back.

And that is where we, the descendants of Ephraim's Ten Tribes, now find ourselves. We recognize that we have followed practices that have displeased God our Father, and we are taking steps to return to him. That is the motivation behind the Torah Awakening. Its roots go very deep into our ancient past, all the way to the days of our first Ephraimite king, Jeroboam son of Nebat:

> Then Jeroboam built Shechem in the hill country of Ephraim, and lived there. And he went out from there and built Penuel. Jeroboam said in his heart, "Now the kingdom will return to the house of David. If this people go up to offer sacrifices in the house of the Lord at Jerusalem, then the heart of this people will return to their lord, *even* to Rehoboam king of Judah; and they will kill me and return to Rehoboam king of Judah." So the king consulted, and made two golden calves, and he said to them, "It is too much for you to go up to Jerusalem; behold your gods, O

Israel, that brought you up from the land of Egypt." He set one in Bethel, and the other he put in Dan. Now this thing became a sin, for the people went *to worship* before the one as far as Dan. And he made houses on high places, and made priests from among all the people who were not of the sons of Levi. Jeroboam instituted a feast in the eighth month on the fifteenth day of the month, like the feast which is in Judah, and he went up to the altar; thus he did in Bethel, sacrificing to the calves which he had made. And he stationed in Bethel the priests of the high places which he had made. Then he went up to the altar which he had made in Bethel on the fifteenth day in the eighth month, even in the month which he had devised in his own heart; and he instituted a feast for the sons of Israel and went up to the altar to burn incense . . . After this event Jeroboam did not return from his evil way, but again he made priests of the high places from among all the people; any who would, he ordained, to be priests of the high places. This event became sin to the house of Jeroboam, even to blot *it* out and destroy *it* from off the face of the earth. (I Kings 12:25-33, 13:33-34)

Jeroboam was not calling Israel to serve foreign gods. He was leading them to serve the Lord in a new way, according to "new revelation" which said they no longer had to follow the Lord's teachings and commandments. The Lord had explained that he would designate a place for all Israel to bring their sacrifices and worship him (Deuteronomy 12:1-14), and that all the men of Israel should appear before him three times each year (Exodus 23:14-17, 34:23). The place God chose was Jerusalem (II Chronicles 6:5-6, 7:16). Thus Jeroboam disregarded the commandment of God and enticed the people of Israel to worship him in different ways. Specifically, Jeroboam instructed Israel:

(1) That it was acceptable to worship the Lord God as an image of a calf, in violation of his commandments not to worship any image (Exodus 20:4-6);

(2) To bring their sacrifices to the new temples to the Lord which Jeroboam built in Dan and Bethel rather than to Jerusalem, the place God had chosen (Deuteronomy 12:1-14; II Chronicles 6:5-6, 7:16);

(3) To celebrate new feast days to the Lord instead of the ones God had specified (Leviticus 23);

(4) To follow the teachings of priests who were not of Levi, the tribe the Lord had chosen as priests (Numbers 18:1-7).

In all these things Jeroboam violated the commandment of the Lord by profaning his Name (Exodus 20:7). Ironically, and tragically, our Israelite ancestors worshipped God, but in ways that seemed good to them, not in the ways he had specified. In so doing they disregarded the Lord's commandments, and that is why he brought judgment on them and exiled them from the Land (I Kings 14:14-16). Every ruler of the Northern Kingdom followed Jeroboam's example. Some, like Ahab, rejected the Lord completely and followed other gods. Others, like Jehu, maintained allegiance to the Lord, but continued to worship him according to the syncretistic practices Jeroboam had institutionalized.

Many of them were effective warriors, diplomats, administrators, and leaders, but by the Lord's standards, every one of them was evil.

It is necessary to heed the lesson of Jeroboam and awaken to the fact that we have continued in his sin. Perhaps it is more understandable if we say that we continue to follow in the sins of Constantine of Rome, who made Israel to sin. The idolatrous practices of both men led their people into great error, being nothing less than changes in times and laws (see Daniel 7:23-27). As Scripture explains, the Lord puts great emphasis on the days he has designated as Appointed Times for his people to meet with him, starting with his Shabbat (Sabbath):

> The Lord spoke to Moses, saying, "But as for you, speak to the sons of Israel, saying, **'You shall surely observe My sabbaths; for *this* is a sign between Me and you throughout your generations, that you may know that I am the Lord who sanctifies you.** Therefore you are to observe the sabbath, for it is holy to you. Everyone who profanes it shall surely be put to death; for whoever does any work on it, that person shall be cut off from among his people. For six days work may be done, but on the seventh day there is a sabbath of complete rest, holy to the Lord; whoever does any work on the sabbath day shall surely be put to death. **So the sons of Israel shall observe the sabbath, to celebrate the sabbath throughout their generations as a perpetual covenant.' It is a sign between Me and the sons of Israel forever**; for in six days the Lord made heaven and earth, but on the seventh day

He ceased *from labor*, and was refreshed."
(Exodus 31:12-17, emphasis added)

Are we not Israel? Indeed yes, as has been demonstrated. Thus the promises and the responsibilities given to Israel from ancient times until now apply to us. We are still subject to the commands God gave to our forefathers at Sinai long ago. Shabbat is to us, just as it was to them, a perpetual covenant, a sign between our God and us. And while we are not going to execute anyone for disregarding the Sabbath (a matter to be discussed later), we understand that forever means forever, and that the unchanging God does not change the way he expects his people to act toward him. Why, then, do we persist in worshipping the Lord on a day dedicated to the sun rather than on the day he set apart as holy? Where in Scripture is it recorded that God moved his holy day from the seventh day of the week to the first day of the week? And where did he change his commandment to rest on that day, permitting his people to do all manner of work or anything they please? As he explained through Isaiah:

If because of the sabbath, you turn your foot from doing your *own* pleasure on My holy day, and call the sabbath a delight, the holy *day* of the Lord honorable, and honor it, desisting from your *own* ways, from seeking your *own* pleasure and speaking *your own* word, then you will take delight in the Lord, and I will make you ride on the heights of the earth; and I will feed you *with* the heritage of Jacob your father, for the mouth of the Lord has spoken. (Isaiah 58:13-14)

But there is more that we do. God specified seven times in the year which we are to observe as his Appointed Times. He summarized them in Leviticus 23, explaining that we should observe these times throughout all our generations as perpetual statutes. These Appointed Times, or Feasts of the Lord, are:

(1) Pesach (Passover), Exodus 12:14.

(2) Matzot (Unleavened Bread), Exodus 12:17.

(3) Firstfruits (more appropriately called Resheet, the Beginning of the Counting of the Omer), Leviticus 23:14.

(4) Shavuot (Pentecost, or Feast of Weeks), Leviticus 23:21, Exodus 34:22, Numbers 28:26.

(5) Yom Teruah (Trumpets, commonly called Rosh Hashanah, the Head of the Year), Numbers 10:8.

(6) Yom Kippur (Day of Atonement), Leviticus 16:29, 31, 23:31.

(7) Sukkot (Tabernacles), Leviticus 23:41.

If the Lord God commanded these holy days, why do we substitute the feast days of pagan gods in place of them? We have taken the feast of the sun god and called it the birthday of our Messiah. We have chosen to honor the day of Messiah's resurrection on the day pagans from time immemorial have honored the fertility goddess known as Ēostre, Ostara, Astarte, Asherah, and many other names. Is it honoring to the Lord God that we take that which is evil and call it good? Is he pleased that we profane his Shabbat even while striving to enter into a fast that pleases him (Isaiah 58:13-14)? Is he pleased that we bow to the gods of our stomachs by eating whatever pleases us, even though he has specified what is food and what is not (Leviticus 11; Isaiah 66:1-7)? These are the hard questions connected with the process of embracing our identity as the returning people of Ephraim.

Instructions from the Apostles

The Lord's admonition is this: come out completely from the idolatry of our ancestors and return to his commandments. The repentance movements have done well thus far, but the time has come to remove ourselves from ignorance and error, as God said through the Apostle Paul:

> Therefore having overlooked the times of ignorance, God is now declaring to men that all *people* everywhere should repent, because He has fixed a day in which He will judge the world in righteousness through a Man whom He has appointed, having furnished proof to all men by raising Him from the dead. (Acts 17:30-31)

Paul preached these words to the people of Athens several years after the Jerusalem Council rendered their judgment about people coming to faith in Yeshua from among the nations. In summarizing the work of the Council, the Apostle James made a highly significant reference to a prophecy by Amos concerning the return of Israel's exiles. James' remarks as recorded in Acts 15 reference only two verses, Amos 9:11-12 (highlighted below), but those verses in context are instructive:

> "Are you not as the sons of Ethiopia to Me, O sons of Israel?" declares the Lord. "Have I not brought up Israel from the land of Egypt, and the Philistines from Caphtor and the Arameans from Kir? Behold, the eyes of the Lord God are on the sinful kingdom, and I will destroy it

from the face of the earth; nevertheless, I will not totally destroy the house of Jacob," declares the Lord. "For behold, I am commanding, and I will shake the house of Israel among all nations as *grain* is shaken in a sieve, but not a kernel will fall to the ground. All the sinners of My people will die by the sword, those who say, 'The calamity will not overtake or confront us.' **In that day I will raise up the fallen booth [tent, tabernacle] of David, and wall up its breaches; I will also raise up its ruins and rebuild it as in the days of old; that they may possess the remnant of Edom and all the nations who are called by My name," declares the Lord who does this.** "Behold, days are coming," declares the Lord, when the plowman will overtake the reaper and the treader of grapes him who sows seed; when the mountains will drip sweet wine and all the hills will be dissolved. Also I will restore the captivity of My people Israel, and they will rebuild the ruined cities and live *in them*; they will also plant vineyards and drink their wine, and make gardens and eat their fruit. I will also plant them on their land, and they will not again be rooted out from their land which I have given them," says the Lord your God. (Amos 9:7-15, emphasis added)

By citing Amos 9, James demonstrated his understanding that the Gentiles coming to faith in Yeshua heralded the restoration of the entire kingdom of Israel under Messiah's reign. The Council's acceptance of James' recommendations demonstrated that the other apostles and elders understood this as well. In fact, they had asked Yeshua about his restoration of the kingdom in their last conversation with him (Acts 1:6). Knowing that the prophecies required all Israel to return to the Torah, and seeing that Yeshua had opened the way, James rendered his judgment that these former Gentiles should have no further burden than to avoid anything contaminated by idols, refrain from sexual immorality, and eat neither blood nor meat from a strangled animal. These four requirements actually embrace a large portion of the Torah's commandments. As stated earlier, James reasoned that they would learn the rest of Torah as they joined with Jews in the synagogues every Shabbat (Acts 15:19-21).

This is quite different from the usual Christian teaching on Acts 15, which holds that the apostles specified only four requirements from the Law which non-Jewish believers in Yeshua were to follow. In actuality, the apostles and elders specified the *minimum requirements* for fellowship with the God of Israel and with his people. The new believers were to turn away from their former pagan lifestyles, which meant no longer participating in the practices that eventually found their way into the Christian celebrations of Christmas and Easter, and the veneration of the day devoted to the sun god. They also were expected to eat only that which God had defined as food, which meant no blood sausages, no pork, and no shellfish. The church in its various manifestations has sought to abide by the standard of avoiding sexual immorality, but the other requirements have been overlooked, ignored, or blatantly disregarded.

A major component in the Ephraimite awakening is the recognition of these errors we have inherited and the understanding that their roots extend back to the practices of our ancient Israelite ancestors. This realization motivates us to depart from the systemic idolatrous practices of our fathers. Because of this, we cannot go back to the church and turn a blind eye to things God has plainly declared are displeasing to him. Yet we also cannot move into some of the customs or religion of Judah, which include the burden of traditions and extra-biblical doctrines the Apostle Peter described as "a yoke which neither our fathers nor we have been able to bear" (Acts 15:10). While we cherish the teaching of Torah from our brethren of Judah, we evaluate each tradition and custom in the light of Scripture to ensure that we do not remove one deviation from the Word of God and replace it with another.

We realize that if we are to see victory, if we are to advance beyond the half-measures and compromises of our past, if we are to fulfill our destiny, then we must humble ourselves before our God and obey his commandments. When we do, he will meet us and instruct us further, and will grant us his blessing and protection. We are in error in many ways. He longs to show us not only our errors, but the way out of them.

We cannot afford to get this wrong. Our fathers and mothers were removed from our homeland because they did these very things. Yet God has promised to bring his people back once we come to our senses and return to him and his ways. Messiah Yeshua has made it possible to return to him, and the Holy Spirit is giving us the new heart the Lord promised so that we can return to his ways. He is restoring our identity through the Torah Awakening, and now he is ready to restore our nationhood. If we are able to govern ourselves in exile according to his commandments, then there is hope that we can govern ourselves in the Land. That, after all, is the purpose of Torah:

> See, I have taught you statutes and judgments just as the Lord my God commanded me, that you should do thus in the land where you are entering to possess it. So keep and do *them*, for that is your wisdom and your understanding in the sight of the peoples who will hear all these statutes and say, "Surely this great nation is a wise and understanding people." For what great nation is there that has a god so near to it as is the Lord our God whenever we call on Him? Or what great nation is there that has statutes and judgments as righteous as this whole law which I am setting before you today? (Deuteronomy 4:5-8)

Our forefathers were not wise and understanding, and we have followed in the footsteps of their foolishness. The nations of the earth have yet to see a people walking consistently in the wise, righteous, just, and merciful statutes and judgments of the Lord God. That is the testimony the Lord requires so that the nations may be drawn to him. He has taken at least six millennia to prepare a people to provide that testimony. The question now is whether that people will heed his call to repentance and walk according to his ways.

---

[1]   A number of ministries and annual events have grown up around the prayer and repentance movement, including the *International House of Prayer*, http://www.ihopkc.org/ (accessed January 31, 2015), *National Day of Prayer*, http://nationaldayofprayer.org/ (accessed January 31, 2015), and *ReignDownUSA*, http://www.reigndownusa.com/ (accessed January 31, 2015). There is even an initiative by the Heartland Apostolic Prayer Network to divorce Baal, meaning to declare a formal break with the idolatrous practices of the past and reaffirm a marriage covenant with the Lord God. Resources related to this initiative are available through the Oklahoma Apostolic Prayer Network at *Divorcing Baal*, http://www.oapn.us/divorcingbaal (accessed January 31, 2015).

4

RECLAIMING THE LAND OF OUR FATHERS

Where Shall We Live?

At the end of the 19th century, when the Zionist Congress began to consider places for a Jewish homeland, they were open to suggestions. Palestine, as the Land of Israel was known at the time, was but one option, albeit first in the hearts of many Zionists. In *Der Judenstaat* (*The Jewish State*), the groundbreaking work that crystallized the Zionist Movement, Theodore Herzl acknowledged the place of Palestine as the historic Jewish homeland. However, Jewish settlement in Palestine required permission from the Sultan of the Ottoman Empire, and the Sultan was not persuaded that permitting Jewish mass migration to Palestine would be in his best interests. Herzl proposed Argentina as an alternative, reasoning that the "Argentine Republic would derive considerable profit from the cession of a portion of its territory to us"[1], but Argentina was not interested in ceding territory to the Jews or to anyone else. In 1903, when the idea arose of settling in the British colony of Uganda, Herzl jumped at the chance, only to see his proposal vehemently opposed at the Sixth Zionist Congress. Although a Zionist delegation investigated settlement possibilities in East Africa, there was never much chance that the Jewish homeland would take shape there. In fact, there really never was any place for the Jews other than the ancient ancestral homeland.

So it is with us. We cannot consider permanent settlement anywhere other than the ancient land promised to our forefathers and to us by the Lord God himself. There is a problem, of course: other people already live on that land. Much of it is already under the sovereignty of the State of Israel, but other portions exist within the current borders of Lebanon, Syria, Jordan, and possibly Egypt. Thus we find ourselves in the same dilemma as the early Zionists: how do we establish our homeland on territory that belongs to someone else?

Before going further I must state emphatically that the Ephraimite Movement has no intention of usurping the sovereignty of any existing state. Regarding the State of Israel in particular, we have no desire to infringe on Israeli territory, nor alter the Jewish nature of the state. We will gladly work with Israel and with the surrounding states to reach accommodation, but only God himself can change existing borders. We take on faith the fact that he will do so in time. His very Name and reputation are at stake because he has promised many times in his Word to resettle us on the land promised to our fathers Abraham, Isaac, and Jacob. We will not move before his time, but when he opens the way we will move, anticipating that God's provision for the current inhabitants of the land will somehow mesh with our needs. We have seen God act in such ways before, not the least being his work in bringing our brethren of Judah to the Land.

When Herzl first penned his vision of the Zionist dream in 1896, the chances of translating that dream into reality were close to zero. Twenty years later, when World War I brought about the disassembly of the Ottoman Empire, British Prime Minister David Lloyd George and Foreign Secretary Arthur Balfour realized that there would be great advantage in promoting a Jewish homeland in the former Ottoman territory. Jewish migration to the Land accelerated under the British Mandate, and before long a nascent Jewish state began to take shape. Later, the upheavals of World War II and the horrors of the Holocaust established the conditions for creation of the State of Israel. It is easy to explain this process by secular means; those who do not expect to see the Hand of God will not be disappointed. Yet those who are looking for him have no difficulty recognizing his direction of events.

There is no need to hide our hope and expectation that the Lord will establish all of our people within the borders he has promised. We do not expect this to happen immediately, and we do not expect that we will all move directly to our promised homeland from the places where we now live. In fact, it could be many years, perhaps even many generations, before this process is complete. We have been waiting over 2,700 years, so a few more decades will not be that great a burden. Yet we require a goal, and there can be no other than what God explained through Ezekiel:

Thus says the Lord God, "This *shall be* the boundary by which you shall divide the land for an inheritance among the twelve tribes of Israel; Joseph *shall have* two portions. You shall divide it for an inheritance, each one equally with the other; for I swore to give it to your forefathers, and this land shall fall to you as an inheritance. This *shall be* the boundary of the land: on the north side, from the Great Sea *by* the way of Hethlon, to the entrance of Zedad; Hamath, Berothah, Sibraim, which is between the border of Damascus and the border of Hamath; Hazer-hatticon, which is by the border of Hauran. The boundary shall extend from the sea *to* Hazar-enan *at* the border of Damascus, and on the north toward the north is the border of Hamath. This is the north side. The east side, from between Hauran, Damascus, Gilead and the land of Israel, *shall be* the Jordan; from the *north* border to the eastern sea you shall measure. This is the east side. The south side toward the south *shall extend* from Tamar as far as the waters of Meribath-kadesh, to the brook *of Egypt and* to the Great Sea. This is the south side toward the south. The west side *shall be* the Great Sea, from the *south* border to a point opposite Lebo-hamath. This is the west side. So you shall divide this land among yourselves according to the tribes of Israel. You shall divide it by lot for an inheritance among yourselves and among the aliens who stay in your midst, who bring forth sons in your midst. And they shall be to you as the native-born among the sons of Israel; they shall be allotted an inheritance with you among the tribes of Israel. And in the tribe with which the alien stays, there you shall give *him* his inheritance," declares the Lord God. (Ezekiel 47:13-23)

Many attempts have been made to draw the map of this "Greater Israel". That is a nice exercise, but at the moment it is too early for maps of any practical consequence. We hardly have a national consciousness as a united people; how can we ask for a homeland before that consciousness is established? Nevertheless, from Ezekiel's prophecy, and from the records of ancient Israel's territorial extent, we glean an idea of the region we should expect to open for us in time.

A Long Journey Home

How shall this land open for us? Most likely the same way such things have always happened: through war and upheaval. This is true not just for Israelites, but for every people which has sought to expand into, or regain, territory. The colonization of the New World provides countless examples, including not only the imperial struggles among the Great Powers of Spain, England, and France, but also the struggles among the American Indian nations. The expansion of the United States to the Pacific Ocean entailed a number of wars, not the least being the Mexican-American War of 1846-48. This is not the place to debate the injustice of those conflicts; every participant has their share of it. These are but examples in the long history of human migrations across this planet. What is important is that great changes in borders and populations happen only through such unhappy means.

Europe is not immune from such phenomena, and in fact provides some of the clearest examples. The nationalist struggles of the 19th and 20th centuries saw the emergence and reemergence of many nation-states based on the claims of various people groups to sovereignty over their ancestral territory. Greece, Germany, and Italy led the way in the nationalist movements of the mid-19th century, inspiring independence movements in Hungary, Serbia, Bulgaria, Romania, Montenegro, Albania, and elsewhere. The greatest example is Poland, a nation which had ceased to exist after being partitioned by its powerful neighbors Austria, Prussia, and Russia in the 1790s. By 1900 it seemed that nothing short of a miracle could restore Poland. And then a miracle happened: World War I resulted in the dissolution of the German, Austro-Hungarian, and Russian empires, and thus a reunited, independent Poland rejoined the community of nations. That same conflict established or confirmed the independence of many other European states, many of which had won a measure of autonomy over the preceding century. Czechoslovakia, Yugoslavia, Finland, and Ukraine came into existence as sovereign states. Later, at the end of the 20th century, Czechoslovakia and Yugoslavia dissolved into their component parts when nationalist movements reached their logical conclusions. In each of these developments, only the division of Czechoslovakia occurred peacefully.

The same process took place in the Middle East after World War I as the death of the Ottoman Empire spelled the birth of new nations. Western colonialism continued for another generation in the form of the British and French mandates, but in time

World War II compelled the withdrawal of those powers from the region. By 1948, the borders drawn by British and French diplomats in 1919 became, with some modifications, the boundaries of the sovereign states of Egypt, Saudi Arabia, Jordan, Lebanon, Syria, Iraq, Turkey, and Israel.

And now the process has begun all over again. The US invasion of Iraq in 2003 started a chain of events that continued through the Arab Spring of 2011, the Syrian Civil War of 2012, and in 2014 the "ISIS Crisis" of a newly-proclaimed Islamic Caliphate which straddles the borders of Iraq and Syria. War now engulfs the region, with Syria in the throes of a conflict with no end in sight. The Syrian war has already spread to the neighboring states, as Turkey struggles to remain aloof, and Lebanon struggles just to survive. The Great Powers that established the old international order have proven incapable of maintaining it, leaving new power brokers in Russia and Iran to reshape the terrain to their liking. In Iraq, a rump Shi'a government is hard pressed to retain control over a portion of its territory, while the Kurdistan Regional Government walks a tightrope over a minefield in its quest for statehood for another people too long denied a nation of their own. And all the while the State of Israel looks warily on, quite ready and able to defend itself even in the face of international censure.

Is this the great upheaval that provides the opportunity for birth of the Ephraimite nation? Possibly. We know from Scripture that war and tribulation accompany the restoration of Israel to the Land. For millennia God's people have expected that this would happen much sooner than it has transpired. We forget that God does not tie himself to our schedules and timelines. Our ancestors were removed from the Land gradually, over the course of an entire generation in the 8th century BCE. Our brethren of Judah were exiled over a lengthy period of time a century later. Their restoration in recent generations has taken over 150 years, and is not yet complete. All of this has involved war and upheaval, so we should expect nothing different in the process now before us. Whether it is the long-expected Great Tribulation is yet to be seen. What we can say for certain is that Ephraim's restoration will be a process fraught with danger, but certain of success. Our God has promised to restore us even in the midst of the "Time of Jacob's Trouble" (see Jeremiah 30), after which Messiah will reunite us with Judah so that we become one nation again under his dominion. When and how that will come about is as yet unclear, but we can see the outlines of it even now.

Like our brethren of Judah, we can expect many twists and turns in our journey home. Like our ancient ancestors in Egypt, we can expect great opposition and oppression. In fact, that is largely what the war and upheaval are all about. Why would any of us want to leave our current homes when we are settled and comfortable? Our ancestors had no need or desire to leave Egypt, and many Jews today have no need or desire to leave their homes in America and Europe. In the first Exodus, God had to make Egypt uninhabitable, and thus a new Pharaoh arose who was hostile to our ancestors. Egyptian oppression made them cry out for deliverance, and God answered by sending Moses. Even then it was a lengthy process before our Israelite fathers and mothers were ready to move into the Land. A whole generation lived and died along the way. Can we expect our experience to be any different? The Babylonian world system in which we now live is too comfortable for us at the moment, but the time is at hand when that comfort factor will be removed. Whether it is through economic collapse, world war, catastrophic natural disasters, extreme persecution, or a combination of all these things, our homes will become uninhabitable for us. When that happens, we should be prepared to leave and set out on the journey to our new ancient homeland. Some of us may be able to move there directly, settling as citizens of the State of Israel in regions where there is yet room. Most of us, however, will have to find temporary homes, perhaps even for many years, before we reach the Land. That is why the Prophet Jeremiah advised us:

> Set up for yourself roadmarks, place for yourself guideposts; direct your mind to the highway, the way by which you went. Return, O virgin of Israel, return to these your cities. (Jeremiah 31:21)

We should begin to look for stopping points where we can live for a time. The ancient paths of our migration into Central and East Asia, Africa, Europe, the Americas, and Australia and the Pacific are the same paths we will travel on our way back. Eventually we will find a place or places to gather as a people, just as the Lord said:

> "As I live," declares the Lord God, "surely with a mighty hand and with an outstretched arm and with wrath poured out, I shall be king over you. I will bring you out from the peoples and

gather you from the lands where you are scattered, with a mighty hand and with an outstretched arm and with wrath poured out; and I will bring you into the wilderness of the peoples, and there I will enter into judgment with you face to face. As I entered into judgment with your fathers in the wilderness of the land of Egypt, so I will enter into judgment with you," declares the Lord God. "I will make you pass under the rod, and I will bring you into the bond of the covenant; and I will purge from you the rebels and those who transgress against Me; I will bring them out of the land where they sojourn, but they will not enter the land of Israel. Thus you will know that I am the Lord." (Ezekiel 36:33-38)

It is significant that these passages in Jeremiah 31 and Ezekiel 36 are in the very chapters that outline the New Covenant so highly prized in Christian doctrine. The process for us, as for Judah, is just as much spiritual as it is physical. Before Messiah joins us together again as one people, we should make ourselves as ready as we can for his reign. The process has already begun in our hearts as we have sought to return to the terms of his covenants with our people. It will be completed during this journey home. If we understand the words of Ezekiel correctly, the journey will not be entirely pleasant, and certainly not without casualties. Not all our ancestors who left Egypt arrived in the Promised Land; not all our brethren of Judah who left Europe, North Africa, and Iraq arrived in Israel. In fact, many of them did not even get the chance to start the journey. Can we expect any less for ourselves?

Where, then, is this "wilderness of the peoples" where we will gather? It could be in the Saudi desert, where our ancestors originally gathered at Sinai. That is speculation, but who can say what God will do? Another possibility is Kurdistan. We travelled there once, on our way into exile by the hand of the Assyrians. The Kurds now live on the lands of the old Assyrian Empire, and they are our distant kin. Already the Kurds of Iraq provide a haven to hundreds of thousands who have fled the depredations of Syria's civil war and the barbaric cruelties inflicted by the Islamic State. If Christians, Yezidis, and Shi'a Muslims find refuge in Kurdistan, could not the Ephraimites as well? Perhaps we should consider establishing ties with the Kurdish government even now, when we are not refugees, by contributing our skills and resources to help them cope with the humanitarian crisis that threatens to overwhelm them. Perhaps we could contribute in ways to help the Kurds defend their land from those who do not want them to govern it. If we can assist our Kurdish kin now, perhaps they will be inclined to assist us in days to come, when our need arrives.

These are the things we should begin to consider if we are to function as a people worthy of a state.

---

[1] Theodore Herzl, *Der Judenstaat*, English translation (New York: Dover Publications, 1988), 76.

5

REBUILDING OUR FATHERS' NATION

Assembling the Bones

At the moment we are not a people, which is exactly what God decreed to our ancestors. The sentence upon our nation was that we would cease being a people, but the glory of God is that he will bring us back and make us a nation again. The Prophet Hosea spoke this quite clearly:

Yet the number of the sons of Israel will be like the sand of the sea, which cannot be measured or numbered; and in the place where it is said to them, "You are not My people," it will be said to them, "*You are* the sons of the living God." And the sons of Judah and the sons of Israel will be gathered together, and they will appoint for themselves one leader, and they will go up from the land, for great will be the day of Jezreel. (Hosea 1:10-11)

As demonstrated previously, this was no secret to Yeshua's followers in the first century. The apostles Paul and Peter both made specific reference to Hosea's prophecies (see Romans 9:22-26 and I Peter

2:9-10) in explaining why so many Gentiles were coming to faith in Yeshua, and in giving those former Gentiles instructions in how to live (Acts 15:20-21).

It is through this prism of Scripture that we understand the phenomenon of the Torah Awakening in our day. Yet the nation is still unformed, the people still scattered, and the consciousness as a people still the stuff of legends. How can that be changed? Truly it is the process of transforming dry bones into living human beings, of bringing life from death. And that is the business of God. Christians have preached for two millennia about the salvation of souls; now we preach the salvation of a nation, and from that nation the salvation of all nations. To do this we refer to the process explained through Ezekiel:

> The hand of the Lord was upon me, and He brought me out by the Spirit of the Lord and set me down in the middle of the valley; and it was full of bones. He caused me to pass among them round about, and behold, *there were* very many on the surface of the valley; and lo, *they were* very dry. He said to me, "Son of man, can these bones live?" And I answered, "O Lord God, You know." Again He said to me, "Prophesy over these bones and say to them, 'O dry bones, hear the word of the Lord.' Thus says the Lord God to these bones, 'Behold, I will cause breath to enter you that you may come to life. I will put sinews on you, make flesh grow back on you, cover you with skin and put breath in you that you may come alive; and you will know that I am the Lord.'" So I prophesied as I was commanded; and as I

prophesied, there was a noise, and behold, a rattling; and the bones came together, bone to its bone. And I looked, and behold, sinews were on them, and flesh grew and skin covered them; but there was no breath in them. Then He said to me, "Prophesy to the breath, prophesy, son of man, and say to the breath, 'Thus says the Lord God, "Come from the four winds, O breath, and breathe on these slain, that they come to life."'" So I prophesied as He commanded me, and the breath came into them, and they came to life and stood on their feet, an exceedingly great army. Then He said to me, "Son of man, these bones are the whole house of Israel; behold, they say, 'Our bones are dried up and our hope has perished. We are completely cut off.' Therefore prophesy and say to them, 'Thus says the Lord God, "Behold, I will open your graves and cause you to come up out of your graves, My people; and I will bring you into the land of Israel. Then you will know that I am the Lord, when I have opened your graves and caused you to come up out of your graves, My people. I will put My Spirit within you and you will come to life, and I will place you on your own land. Then you will know that I, the Lord, have spoken and done it," declares the Lord.'" (Ezekiel 37:1-14)

We are still hidden in our graves in the Valley of Dry Bones. We are not even recognizable as skeletons, but rather as scattered bones and pieces of bones. Some, like the Lemba of Southern Africa and the Bnei Menashe of India, can at least define themselves as communities, but most of us cannot even say that much. Many of us have left our affiliation with organized Christianity, and are reevaluating our national identity, but as yet the national Israelite identity of Ephraim remains only in its infancy.

And so it will remain until we decide to make it more than a vision. This is humanly impossible, but with God nothing is impossible. The question is whether we will do our part. When he did the impossible of bringing Messiah into this world, he did so with willing human partners: a young woman ready to do her part as an unwed mother, and a young man ready to marry her and raise the Son of God as his own. So it is with us. God is ready to bring this nation into existence, and as the Scripture explains, it is only his Spirit that will breathe life into it. Our part is to bring the bones into some semblance of order.

The Power of Symbols

A nation needs a people, a language, a territory, a name, a flag, a government, and a body of laws. We know who the people are: they are us, the people ready to be recognized as Ephraimites, reassembling ourselves from the vast sea of humanity in every nation on earth. We are of no single ethnicity; our skin colors are as varied as the entire human race. That is the beauty of God's kingdom of Israel. From the very beginning it has included people of varied ethnicity. Our ancestors married Syrians, Egyptians, Canaanites, Moabites, and others willing to trade the identity of their birth for the identity of Israel. Our very diversity speaks to the grace and glory of our God, and our ability to live and work together testifies of his transforming power. But first we have to think of ourselves as one people. And that is the beginning of this miracle.

We are of no single language. The tongues of our birth have served us well to this point, but we require a uniform speech that we can call our own. This question of language may be the one with the easiest answer. In truth, we have only one answer: Hebrew, the language of our ancestors. We owe an incalculable debt to our brethren of Judah for restoring Hebrew to life as a modern language. All of us who aspire to be citizens of our new nation (including this author) should make a concerted effort to learn Hebrew so that we may communicate freely. We can rely on major international languages like English, Spanish, Arabic, French, Russian, Mandarin, Hindi, and others to help us along, but the utmost educational priority for the emerging Ephraimite nation is instruction in Hebrew. Language study provides us with a ready-made program to bring us together as communities. It should be relatively easy to engage instructors from Jewish community centers, universities, online courses, and native speakers from our brethren of Judah. In time Hebrew will become the chief language of our national congresses, our national press, and our national life.

The best way to learn any language is by immersion – constant use of the language in daily activities. Our success in this endeavor will be determined by our ability to build Hebrew-speaking communities in the nations where we now live. This is more than just a collection of people connected by congregational affiliation who see each other only in the context of a religious gathering. It is community with a consciousness of being a community: people living and working together, fellowshipping with one another, and interacting in every way that people encounter each other in their daily lives. This is not such a strange thing. Our Jewish brethren have lived so for centuries, as have many other peoples living among alien cultures. It is in community that we build Ephraimite culture. Many, and perhaps most, of us are now isolated from one another, not sure where to turn for fellowship, encouragement, instruction, and assurance that we are not alone. Thanks to the internet we are even now building virtual communities through live streaming Hebrew Roots Torah teaching and worship, email, blogs, teleconferences, and more. There are already many gatherings of like-minded believers at Sukkot in various places. This is a very good start, but it is time to consider how to transform these virtual communities into actual communities. That means many of us will have to relocate so that we can live near fellow Ephraimites. Initially this relocation and community building should happen in the lands we now call home. We should look for places where we can congregate as neighbors and learn to live together as a distinct people. Perhaps this means establishing new villages and towns in rural areas, or perhaps moving into neighborhoods in cities and suburbs where housing is available. When we look we will find many possibilities. The important thing is to look, to make a concerted effort to find one another, associate with one another, live next to one another, and together create the meaning of the Ephraimite people. And what better way to do that than by learning Hebrew together, both by studying and speaking Modern Hebrew, and by discovering the deeper meanings of the Scripture in the original Biblical Hebrew.

To enhance our language skills and to build our national consciousness we could add programs to acquaint our people with their homeland. We already know the location of our homeland, and although large portions of it are not open to us now, the heart of it is accessible. Our Jewish brethren have fulfilled much of the prophecies regarding the return of all our people, and they have regained control of the city that will be our national capital when Messiah reunites us one day. Let us establish programs to visit the State of Israel, not as tourists, but as exiles longing to return to the land of our fathers. There is a model already: the Taglit-Birthright Israel Foundation brings thousands of Jewish youth to the Land each year to acquaint them with their heritage and their people. We should establish a similar Ephraimite Birthright Foundation that will serve the same purpose for our young people. At the same time, we require programs for older Ephraimites just now becoming aware of their heritage. The youth are our future, but the older generations are our present, and we should educate both if we are to create a national consciousness. Let us bring them to the Land to walk the places where our ancestors walked. Let them see Jerusalem, where our God has placed his Name. Let them see as well Shomron (Samaria), Dan, and Bethel, where our fathers rebelled against God and incurred his wrath. We should teach them the full story so that we do not repeat the errors of our past, but instead move forward in the path of life and blessing marked by the Torah of the Living God.

As we learn our language and learn our land, we need to find a way to share our experiences and views with one another. For that we need a national press. We require willing and able correspondents, editors, publicists, scholars, and translators who can view global events, analyze them in terms of their impact on the Ephraimite people, and report their findings. The advantages of the internet and mass audio and video communications will aid our cause immeasurably. Thanks to these modern technological miracles, we can do in a month what our Zionist forebears required ten years to accomplish. This is how we build our national consciousness, and how we acquaint the world with our existence. We can do it much better than anyone has done before. No other people group or organization has the advantage we have: we come from every nation and tribe and tongue on earth, and thus within our national body are members who understand the way to communicate within every cultural context. Together we can craft messages that influence while avoiding the pitfalls of miscommunication.

By these measures we will see our people, our language, our territory, and our message come into focus, but there is something fundamental that we require to bring them all together. We need a name, and we need a national symbol. These are matters of debate which can only be resolved by consensus. However, we need a starting point for that debate. For that reason, I propose the following.

Let us consider calling our nation *The Ephraimite State of Northern Israel.* In common reference we may refer to our nation as Northern Israel. That may sound strange to the ear, but it is no more strange than the names of other nations divided into two parts. Today the world is quite familiar with North and South Korea, and in recent memory has known North and South Vietnam, North and South Yemen, and East and West Germany. We require a name that distinguishes our nation from the current State of Israel, but which identifies us as Israelite and kin to the Jewish state. While it would be convenient for the State of Israel to be renamed Judah, such a change would be impractical and unreasonable. Therefore we should create a suitable name which communicates to the world that we are the fulfillment of our God's promises, and that we are ready to reclaim our place as a people. Until Messiah comes and unites us under his reign, Northern Israel will suffice.

Our nation's flag should represent our identity and calling. A proposed design has at its center a field of black, the color of the House of Joseph according to the onyx stone for Joseph in the breastplate of the High Priest (Exodus 28:15-20). On the field are twelve Stars of David (*Magen David*) representing the Twelve Tribes of Israel – not just the Ten Lost Tribes, but the portions of Judah included among them (Joseph and his companions; Ezekiel 37:15-28). These are six-pointed Stars of David which testify to our returning allegiance to the House of David, thus ending the rebellion of our fathers recorded in I Kings 12:16-19. The twelve stars surround a larger Star which represents the Son of David, Messiah the Prince who commands our loyalty and who will one day reunite us with our brethren of Judah. This pattern of stars recalls the two dreams of our father Joseph, who foresaw that his brothers would bow down to him (Genesis 37:5-11), and testifies to Messiah Yeshua's fulfillment of both roles as *Moshiach ben Yosef* (Messiah Son of Joseph) and *Moshiach ben David* (Messiah Son of David). On either side of the black field with the star pattern are thin vertical stripes of white, speaking to the purification of the saints of God through the redeeming work of Messiah. Outside the white stripes are wider vertical stripes of royal blue which remind us of the Law of our God (Numbers 15:37-41) and our calling into a priestly kingdom (Exodus 19:5-6; I Peter 2:4-10; Revelation 1:4-8, 5:9-10).

Matters of Substance

Our efforts at building a national consciousness and at translating that consciousness into a nation state require considerable resources. Here is another endeavor in which we may look to our Jewish brethren for a model. The Jewish National Fund established by the Fifth Zionist Congress in 1901 provided the funds for much of the Zionist program, including buying land in Ottoman-occupied Palestine and assisting Jewish families in making *Aliyah*. We require a similar fund or funds for our efforts. Land acquisition is not our priority at the moment, but in time it will be. For now we require funds for education and to build national institutions like culture centers, embassies, media outlets, and regional headquarters. Soon we will need full-time workers devoted to these efforts. We will also need funds to assist Ephraimites in difficult straits, helping them to find food, clothing, shelter, legal assistance, medical attention, and resettlement. Those in wealthier nations should be willing to bear a greater share of the burden, but all should contribute as they are able. In this is the opportunity to form habits based on the commandments of our God, such as not charging interest to our brethren, and caring for the poor, the widows, and the fatherless among us. This is not a utopian endeavor free from accountability; it is a Torah-based effort conducted with complete transparency and in line with the laws of the nations that are now our homes. While tax-exempt status is tempting, we should scrutinize every possibility to ensure that we do not incur ties, bonds, or obligations that encumber our freedom of action and our integrity before God. Thus, we should not be afraid to render unto Caesar the things that belong to Caesar by paying taxes and abiding by existing laws and regulations.

As we abide by the laws and regulations of our host nations, we develop laws and regulations applicable to our distinct communities. For that we require a governing body or bodies. Ultimately our nation shall be a monarchy, ruled by God himself dwelling among us. Until then, we hold the land and people in trust, governing ourselves in his Name and according to his laws. While this is yet a matter of debate, perhaps years from realization, I propose that the best form of government for our nation is parliamentary. Every adult citizen may vote, and their votes shall elect representatives to a parliament to serve as the elders at our gates. These parliamentarians will elect a prime minister to oversee the government in the Name of the King, looking continuously to his Torah as the standard for our national laws, policies, and conduct. What we call this parliament is yet to be decided. Since we will be a Hebrew-speaking people, perhaps Knesset is suitable.

There is no urgency on the matter of naming our parliament, but there is urgency in the establishment of an Ephraimite National Congress, or other suitable bodies, that can begin to speak for us. The Zionist Congresses of the last century gave birth to the World Zionist Organization, World Zionist Congress, and Jewish Agency, which exert powerful influence over the lives and fate of Jews across the globe. We require something like this. The beginning may be small, but we begin nevertheless by gathering as many as can come to represent Ephraimites from as many nations and communities and congregations as possible. This gathering shall establish a governing body to oversee the work of building this nation. The officers of the Ephraimite Congress should have sufficient powers to represent the national community, to establish guidelines, policies, and procedures, and to raise and oversee the expenditure of funds for national development and other needs. Every officer should be selected according to biblical standards, just as Jethro advised Moses:

> Furthermore, you shall select out of all the people able men who fear God, men of truth, those who hate dishonest gain; and you shall place *these* over them *as* leaders of thousands, of hundreds, of fifties and of tens. Let them judge the people at all times; and let it be that every major dispute they will bring to you, but every minor dispute they themselves will judge. So it will be easier for you, and they will bear *the burden* with you. If you do this thing and God *so* commands you, then you will be able to

endure, and all these people also will go to their place in peace. (Exodus 18:21-23)

This is not a gendered proposition. Women can and must serve in our leadership structures, just as biblical examples have taught us. Deborah, our foremother, judged all Israel, and we do well to remember her example. So, too, do we remember the admonition of the Apostle Paul, that in Messiah Yeshua there is no distinction of male or female in terms of equality (Galatians 3:28).

This, then, is our program for building a people into a nation and a state. How long will it take? Perhaps much less time than we might expect. But even now it is wise to consider what our society will look like and how we will act as a people determined to adopt the commandments of our God as the defining standard of our national existence.

6

LIVING AMONG OUR FATHERS' KIN

Speaking Comfortably to Jerusalem

Miraculous. Radical. Threatening. These and many more descriptive terms apply to this rebirth of the Ephraimite nation. What fills some hearts with thrill and hope strikes suspicion and fear in other hearts. There is no way we can avoid offense, for our very existence threatens the definition of the current world structure. For millennia that structure has consisted essentially of two groups: Jews and everyone else. Jews are Israel and Israel is Jewish, or so the conventional understanding has been since the Assyrians carried away our ancestors. The rest of the world is Gentile, a category divided into many subcategories, such as Christian, Muslim, Hindu, or atheist. Anything which challenges this world order is a threat not only to Jews, but also to every people group that defines itself in some way as *not Jewish*.

Christians and Muslims especially have taken great pains to define themselves in opposition to Judaism and anything Jewish, even to the point of making war on Jews. There is little that Ephraimites can do to change Muslim attitudes, particularly those of extremists who seek to impose an Islamic order of their own definition on the entire population of the earth. We will seek to live in peace with Muslims, but it is inevitable that many within the realm of Islam will consider us their mortal enemies. Israel is their mortal enemy, and up to now they have reasoned that the global population of their enemy is around 14 million Jews. What will be the reaction when millions more Israelites identify themselves as such and begin to make a concerted effort at returning to their ancient homeland? The answer is clear; we should expect that the terrorist methods employed against our brethren of Judah will be directed against us also. If the treatment of the State of Israel in the United Nations and the world press is any indication, we should expect enemies at every turn simply because of who we are.

In similar ways we present a threat to Christians of every sect. We challenge the prevailing notion that the church is distinct from Israel, that Jesus abolished the Law of Moses, and that heaven is the exclusive reward for believers in Jesus. Centuries of Replacement Theology have resulted in a spectrum of anti-Semitic attitudes across Christendom. At the extreme end of that spectrum are those in the church who question Israel's (meaning the Jews') right to the Land, and who champion the cause of Arab extremists who seek to eliminate the State of Israel. At the other end are Christian Zionists who support Israel (meaning the Jews) and want to see the State of Israel victorious in all conflicts with its enemies, but who believe that they will leave this earth to the Jews when Jesus comes to take them away to heaven.

These are, of course, over-simplified descriptions; the attitudes within Christendom are quite varied and nuanced, and this is not the place to investigate them thoroughly. All we require for the moment is to be aware of how Christendom will react to our presence.

We are already beginning to see that reaction. The Torah Awakening is now to the point that it is generating more than mere curiosity and tolerance among traditional Christians. We threaten their traditions, from the family gathering at Christmas to the time-honored obligation of Sunday worship. Eventually this will translate into economic impact as more and more Hebrew Roots believers cease buying pork products, stop going out to eat on Friday evenings, withdraw from Saturday sports and other events, and seek employment at jobs that permit them to observe Shabbat and the Feasts of the Lord. While it is unfair to paint all Christians with a broad brush, we should look realistically at this situation. Not all Christians are Spirit-filled, Bible-believing, tolerant, loving individuals who seek the Lord first above all things. Many are Christians in name only, and thus cannot be counted on to act in good faith as Jesus would have acted. Others are sincere believers, but their lives revolve around what their church traditions teach them the Scripture says rather than what the Scripture actually says. Such people, however kind and good, are not easily persuaded to change their understanding, or even to look at Scriptural challenges to their beliefs. These are the realities that generated the darkest parts of church history: the Crusades, forced conversions of indigenous peoples, pogroms and expulsions of Jews, and turning a blind eye toward the Holocaust. Our hope will always be that our shared faith in and loyalty to Messiah Yeshua will provide sufficient grounds for fellowship and cooperation with our Christian brethren, but we should be prepared for opposition not only to our theological understandings, but to our efforts at restoring a nation whose existence will challenge the core of their beliefs about the world and God's relationship to mankind.

Yet the greatest potential opposition we face is not from Christians or Muslims, but from our own kin: our brethren of Judah. This includes not only the religious Jews of all persuasions who do not acknowledge Yeshua of Nazareth as Messiah, but also many Messianic Jews who are reluctant at best to admit that there is another part of Israel which is not Jewish. It is the division with our Messianic brethren that I will address first. These are the very people whom the Lord has used to bring us non-Jews closer to the full truth of Scripture. The Torah Awakening would not have occurred if it were not for them. Even now many Messianic Jewish brethren labor tirelessly, both in the Land and in the Diaspora, to proclaim the good news of salvation in Yeshua, often under extreme danger to their livelihood, their reputations, and their very lives. We applaud these efforts and we pray for the continued success of the many good works they have done. And yet we appeal to our Messianic brethren to look again at what Scripture says about the Two Houses of Israel. How can it be that the Two Houses, Judah and Ephraim, are contained fully within the Jewish people? How is it possible that the many prophecies of the return of all Israel to the Land speak only to the return of the Jews? If that is so, why is the State of Israel not yet organized along tribal lines? Indeed, where are the tribes which Ezekiel and the Apostle John said would be back in the land as tribes? Who among the Jewish people are the Ephraimites, the descendants of Joseph and the other tribes? These are but a few of the many questions we would ask in hope that we may reason together and find ways to live and work together in peace. Surely we can find common ground in the fact that together we share the testimony of Yeshua and the Commandments of God.

The Commandments of God form the common ground we share with all observant Jews, even those who reject Yeshua. There is no hiding the fact that Yeshua's claims to be Messiah, and to be the Son of God, cause offense to most Jews, and for that reason we, too, are an offense because of our beliefs. We cannot compromise on this, but at the same time we remember what Yeshua himself said: that it is only the Father in heaven who reveals the identity of Messiah (Matthew 16:15-18). Our intent, therefore, is not to "convert" Jews to faith in Yeshua. Our intent is to appeal for peaceful cooperation and understanding in that we share a faith in the God of Abraham, Isaac, and Jacob, and that we construct our lives around the Scriptures that he has given to mankind. No one can deny the essential Jewishness either of Yeshua or of the disciples who carried his message to the world in the first century. If we are correct in believing Yeshua to be Messiah, then God will reveal that to our Jewish brethren in time. For now, we share a belief that God will send his Messiah to earth, and we can learn much from one another about who this Messiah is and what he will do. In the meantime, we should be able to cooperate on the basis of our mutual identity as Hebrews.

And yet it is our Hebraic identity that may draw the greatest opposition from the very people who can help us the most. A persistent Jewish expectation throughout the ages has been the return of the House of Ephraim. Many sages have pondered the question of where the Lost Tribes are and when and how they will return. The underlying expectation is that the Lost Tribes will return as Jews to Judaism. What we present is something entirely different: the Lost Tribes returning not as Jews, and not to Judaism, but as Torah-observant believers in Yeshua. This is not only a challenge to conventional Jewish understanding and expectations, but also a threat to the very definition of the Jewish identity and religion. If "Jewish" means only a part of the Hebrew or Israelite nation, then Jews risk losing their status in that nation and their sole proprietorship of it. It is no wonder, then, that our brethren of Judah view our return with suspicion at best.

The world has seen this before. This very dynamic fueled the controversy about Yeshua and his followers in the first century. Jews rightly viewed themselves and their nation as the means by which God would bring salvation into the world, but the way God chose to do that did not match Jewish expectations. Salvation meant conversion to Judaism and identification with Israel, which was in those days the Jewish nation. As the book of Acts explains, the gospel of the kingdom which the apostles preached did not include a requirement to convert to Judaism, and therein came the controversy. The believers in Yeshua were already in opposition to the Jewish leadership of the various sects and of the Temple because they recognized the authority of Scripture over the doctrinal interpretations of the Pharisees and Sadducees. When these believers began accepting Gentiles into their circle without immediate circumcision and complete conversion to Judaism, the opposition intensified and widened. Factions within the body of believers contended that these former Gentiles had to be circumcised and become Jews in order to be saved, regardless what they professed about Yeshua. That was the very reason for the Council of Jerusalem (see Acts 15), and the motivation behind Paul's letter to the Galatians. We know from history how that controversy turned out. There was no solution; eventually the non-Jewish believers in Yeshua separated from the Jewish believers, and over time positions hardened as Christianity and Judaism became distinct and mutually antagonistic religious systems. In a spiritual sense, it was a reenactment of the rebellion of Ephraim against King Rehoboam. And so Israel remains in rebellion against the House of David to this day.

We must heal this breach. Actually, God himself will heal the breach, but we have our part to do. That means we Ephraimites should reach out in respect and love to our older brother Judah. The Apostle Paul explained that it is the Jews who have the oracles of God (Romans 3:1-2), and that to them belong the adoption as sons, the glory and the covenant, the giving of the Law, the Temple service, the promises, the fathers, and even Messiah himself (Romans 9:1-5). No matter how our Jewish brethren perceive and act toward us, we should always act in love toward them and defer to them on these matters. This is, in fact, what Yeshua told us:

> Then Jesus spoke to the crowds and to His disciples, saying: "The scribes and the Pharisees have seated themselves in the chair of Moses; therefore all that they tell you, do and observe, but do not do according to their deeds; for they say *things* and do not do *them*." (Matthew 23:1-3)

Let us not make too much, nor too little, of this instruction. There is much in modern Judaism that is admirable and which we should emulate. Yet there is much that we should scrutinize and question in the light of Scripture. It is true that Jewish sages have been the most renowned authorities on the Torah and the other books of the Tanakh (Old Testament), and we do well to take their teachings into consideration. No one else knows the original language or the extra-biblical Hebraic sources any better than these Jewish authorities. Moreover, when the Temple is rebuilt and the priesthood reinstated, Jews will do it. We will support these efforts, and we will seek to participate in them by contributing our offerings and drawing near to worship at the Temple, but the priesthood is of the tribe of Levi, and the Levites for the most part are of the House of Judah.

We do not seek to usurp the rightful place of our Jewish brethren in these key functions. Nevertheless, we assert our own place as men and women of Israel who have minds of our own and the ability, with help from the Holy Spirit, to understand and interpret Scripture for ourselves. What we ask is that we may have a part in the discussion. We respect rabbinical authority and appreciate the place of the rabbis.

When our nation is formed we will need rabbinical assistance in interpreting the fine points of Torah. However, we respectfully request that our voice be heard as well. We come to the table with two millennia of Christian teaching which has something of value to contribute, but we come as Hebrews who have departed from the idolatrous practices that have infused themselves into Christian tradition. Surely the effort we have made to come out of such error is worthy of consideration. On that basis we ask our brethren of Judah to accept us as fellow Hebrews.

A Pragmatic Approach to Judah

There is one other element of the House of Judah which deserves our attention: traditional Jews. Perhaps these are the largest part of the Jewish people. They are Jewish by the recognized criteria, but do not necessarily hold Jewish religious beliefs even though they generally keep Jewish traditions. Many of these men and women are the politicians, lawyers, medical professionals, engineers, scientists, farmers, and other professionals with whom we shall work to establish our nation. To them our claims of Israelite identity are the stuff of myth and legend. Those who live in the West do not care whether we call ourselves Israelites or Martians, and have little inclination to bother about our existence and activities. But those who live in the State of Israel have every reason to take notice of us. Specifically, are we a threat to the Jewish State? Do we seek to supplant them by making Israel something other than the Jewish Homeland? Or are we, perhaps, allies like the Christians Zionists whose support can be leveraged to Israel's advantage?

We are allies. It is not our desire to remake the State of Israel, to change its demographics, or to redefine it as anything but Jewish. That is why we seek a separate state of our own on territory not under the sovereignty of the State of Israel. Although it might be theoretically possible to establish some kind of Ephraimite territory within the borders of Israel, such a thing is neither practical nor desirable. Israelis would interpret calls for such a territory as yet another demand for Jewish land. That is unacceptable, for we see the State of Israel not as our enemy, but as our dearest friend and brother. Some of us have already taken up residence within Israel, and more will come. These will never be more than a small fraction of the many millions of Ephraimites worldwide, but they will fulfill an indispensable role as our ambassadors to Judah. They will live among our brethren and help us communicate effectively with them. They will advise us how to plead our case as fellow Israelites, and as willing allies ready to help secure the State of Israel as an essential part of securing a state of our own. And indeed this may be the greatest argument we have in persuading our brethren. In ancient days, the Northern Kingdom served as a buffer, shielding Judah from the worst of the threats from hostile neighbors in Syria and Mesopotamia. It is true that ancient Judah and Israel frequently warred against one another, and seldom were their relations friendly. Nevertheless, as long as Northern Israel existed, Judah enjoyed a greater measure of security. The same can happen in our time. When we have a land of our own, we can serve as a buffer against threats to Israel from the north and east. Together with our brethren we can stand back to back, looking out for one another's safety, security, and welfare.

Even before we have a land of our own, our people of all ages could perform a wide variety of functions for our brethren. We will gladly send volunteers to live for short periods in Israel and serve as laborers in agriculture and industry, in support of the Israel Defense Forces, and in other ways. In this way we would contribute to Israel's prosperity and security, learn the customs and language, and demonstrate through selfless acts of devotion that our intentions are pure. Indeed, it is by humble service more than by clever arguments that we will win the confidence of our Jewish brethren.

Walking Together In Agreement

It is in humility that we approach this entire process, beginning with our dealings among ourselves. We cannot persuade Judah, nor Christendom, nor any other part of humanity that we are worthy of consideration if we cannot achieve consensus on matters that now divide us. That which should unite us is our testimony of Yeshua as Messiah and our adherence to the Commandments of God. And yet it is our various interpretations of his Commandments that have left us fragmented. Although we agree on the commandments to observe the Feasts of the Lord, we cannot yet agree on which calendar to follow so that we may observe his Feasts together. There is even disagreement on whether Shabbat falls on the seventh day of the week consistently, or changes with each New Moon. Then there are disputes about how to pronounce the Sacred Name, YHVH, and even how to write and pronounce the Name of our Messiah. Some wear *tzittzit*, and some do not, and those who do debate whether to wear them outside their clothing or inside. Some keep kosher to the extreme, observing the customs of *kashrut* as strictly as any Orthodox Jew, while others eat a biblically clean diet according to the specifications of Leviticus 11 and do not concern themselves with such things as separating meat from dairy. The disagreements go on and on, to the point of the ridiculous.

If we are to build this nation, we have to find a way to accommodate our differences. Unless and until the Holy Spirit simultaneously zaps our collective consciousness with a uniform understanding of the Scripture, our only recourse on certain matters is compromise and consensus. There is a place for compromise, just as the apostles and elders demonstrated when they wrestled with the issue of Gentiles coming into the kingdom. Again we refer to the example of Acts 15. All recognized the standard: God established Torah as his way for us to live, and those coming into the faith from among the Gentiles needed to learn and follow Torah. The compromise which resulted in consensus was to specify the four minimum requirements for these new believers, with the understanding that they would learn Torah in time and that with help from the Holy Spirit they would modify their lifestyles accordingly. The extreme positions in this debate were not satisfied: the Pharisees did not get their way in that the new believers were not circumcised immediately; and those who would have excused the former Gentiles from continued instruction in Torah were likewise disappointed. Some among each faction may have chosen not to remain in fellowship with the majority, but the consensus prevailed and the body of believers continued to mature and grow.

So it should be with us. We will disagree, but in our disagreement let us continue to fellowship with one another, pray with and for one another, and together seek the full revelation of that which we do not completely understand. We should view our disagreements as opportunities to push on in love, trusting the Holy Spirit to work out the details. Love is indeed the means of covering all manner of offense as we wait for the Spirit to work. It is the hardening of hearts and attitudes that makes it impossible for him to work and which will keep us in the Valley of Dry Bones. We will err, for we are still imperfect in our understanding and practice of God's ways. But when we err we will err as a nation, and when the Holy Spirit reveals our error, we will repent as a nation. That is the difference between us and our ancestors, both of Israel and of the nations into which we have been scattered.

In this attitude of love, I propose a starting point for our national consensus. So that we may be in agreement with the majority of our brethren of Judah, let us adopt officially the Jewish Calendar developed by Hillel II which is currently in use throughout the Jewish world. It is widely understood that this calendar is imperfect, and there are good reasons why Karaite Jews and many Messianic and Hebrew Roots believers do not abide by it. However, until there is a new Temple, priesthood, and Sanhedrin to decide these matters and determine the manner of calculating the New Moon each month, we have need of a single means of measuring time for our nation. Adopting the Hillel II Calendar is the best means available to us. Our adoption of this calendar for our national purposes does not prevent individuals and groups from observing New Moons, Feasts, and Shabbats according to their preferred manner of calculation. Nor does it keep us from changing to one of these methods as the Lord corrects our national understanding.

The calendar question is but one of many that we will need to consider. What we are doing here is nothing less than applying God's Torah to our national character. Jews have sought to do this for much, much longer than we, and thus we do not lightly dismiss their practices and doctrines. However, we are approaching this process from a new direction and with a fresh perspective. It is our desire to comply with Torah that defines our very identity even more than it defines the identity of most Jews. Most certainly it will define our Ephraimite nation differently from the Jewish State of Israel. The state our Jewish brethren have built is Jewish in character and culture, but it is not a godly nation. Israel is a secular nation-state, albeit one built on some of the best products of political development since the Enlightenment. Our state will not be secular, but based on Torah. Our dilemma is how to translate Torah into national policy. I cannot solve that dilemma in this short work; the best I can do is to describe parameters under which the questions may be addressed by others more qualified than I.

The proposition of using Torah as the basis of our community ordinances and national laws will meet with immediate opposition from those who do not understand. The prevailing opinion of the "Old

Testament laws" holds that they are harsh and merciless. How else would a modern person describe provisions for capital punishment by stoning, or death penalties for disobedience to parents, witchcraft, and homosexuality? Yet the casual observer does not understand the nature of the Law. God explains his perfect standard, but he also explains his high regard for love, mercy, and justice. His Law is one of due process, requiring multiple witnesses to any matter, calling on wise, righteous judges to investigate every matter thoroughly, and offering every accused offender the opportunity for a defense and to repent of any wrongdoing. This is no arbitrary justice according to the letter of the law, which, as Paul says, brings death (II Corinthians 3:4-6). It is application of the Law of God as the Prophet Micah explained: doing justice, loving kindness, and walking humbly with our God (Micah 6:8). Yeshua echoed this instruction, identifying justice, mercy, and faithfulness as the weightier provisions of the Law (Matthew 23:23). By these instructions from Scripture we understand that the defining characteristic of a Torah-observant society is not uncompromising legalism, but a continuous effort at balancing justice and mercy so that the love of God may find practical expression.

Let us begin even now, among ourselves, to apply these Torah principles of justice, mercy, and faithfulness in our dealings with one another while we live out what we understand of God's ways. By cultivating habits based on these principles we will become the wise and understanding people our King wants us to be.

EPILOGUE

WHEN EGYPT BECOMES
UNINHABITABLE

Up to this point in time the issues raised in this work have resided in the realm of legend and fancy. Those who bothered to think about the Ten Lost Tribes of Israel usually considered them nothing more than a vanished people of antiquity. Very few gave the Lost Tribes any serious thought, and even those who investigated their existence usually did so in the context of tracing the paths they might have traveled into exile. Hardly anyone considered that they might still exist, and that they might one day become a nation again. To think such a thing would be ludicrous at best. The tribes of Ephraim have not existed as a national entity for over 2,700 years. How could one hope that they might be resurrected in this modern age?

Yet that is precisely what we hope. More than that, it is precisely what we expect. We are taking what has until now been nothing more than a theoretical discussion within a series of theological debates and treating it as a serious proposition. We are doing nothing less than investigating the political, diplomatic, economic, ethnographic, security, logistics, and legal issues involved in creating an autonomous nation on inhabited hostile territory within the borders of existing states. Such a proposition is beyond ludicrous; it is madness.

How very much like the Most High God to do such a thing. And indeed that is our hope; if God is not in this, we are beyond hope and pity. But if this is what the Lord God meant in the most extensive subject addressed by his prophets and apostles, we would be fools not to take him at his word.

Let us think for a moment about the situation of our ancestors in Egypt 3,500 years ago. Surely they were aware of the promises God had made to their father Abraham:

> Now when the sun was going down, a deep sleep fell upon Abram; and behold, terror and great darkness fell upon him. God said to Abram, "Know for certain that your descendants will be strangers in a land that is not theirs, where they will be enslaved and oppressed four hundred years. But I will also judge the nation whom they will serve, and afterward they will come out with many possessions. As for you, you shall go to your fathers in peace; you will be buried at a good old age. Then in the fourth generation they will return here, for the iniquity of the Amorite is not yet complete." (Genesis 15:12-16)

By the time of Moses' birth, the prophesied period of 400 years was nearing completion. Moses may even have been motivated by the prophecy when, at the age of 40, he murdered an Egyptian who was oppressing a fellow Israelite. Some 390 years had transpired to that point. It is possible that Moses, anticipating the imminent redemption of Israel, sought to hasten events by asserting his claim as an advocate and protector of the people. The actual deliverance did not occur until 40 years later, exactly 430 years from the day God spoke to Abraham. Even after that another 40 years would pass before the people were ready to enter and possess the Promised Land. What we learn from the accounts in Exodus, Leviticus, Numbers, and Deuteronomy is that the people of Israel had a very hard time dealing with that process. They were expecting a Bronze Age version of instant gratification, meaning that they expected God to transplant them without delay from Egypt into Canaan so that they could live happily ever after.

Things did not work out quite like that. First of all, circumstances had to develop that would render Egypt uninhabitable for the Israelites. That is why a "new king" arose in Egypt who oppressed the people, causing them to cry out to the Lord for deliverance. No doubt their prayers included petitions to change Pharaoh's heart, to return Egypt to the way it had been in the days of their fathers, when worship of the Lord God was at least tolerated and his people permitted to live in peace in their adopted land. The people by that time had been in the land for generations. They had known no other home, and the prospect of leaving Egypt never entered the mind of many. Their expectation was that God would make Egypt a happy place for them once more if they could repent thoroughly enough and influence Egypt for good rather than allow wicked people to hijack their homeland.

God answered their prayers, but not in the way they anticipated. Some among the Hebrews no doubt remembered the promises to father Abraham, and in remembering those promises they began to remind God that he had declared his intent to take them out of their foreign exile into the Promised Land. Those were the prayers God was ready to answer, for the time had come to fulfill his promises. Yet even then his answers did not match entirely with his people's expectations. Moses himself, the great Prince of Egypt who expected to lead his people in triumphant conquest, required a great deal of processing before he was ready to be God's instrument of deliverance. That was the purpose of his 40 years on the backside of the desert. And even after that, when deliverance happened, it was lengthy and painful. The people had to endure ten grievous plagues as God judged Egypt. Although the Lord protected them from the worst of the plagues, they still had to watch as their friends, neighbors, and even family members suffered immeasurably. Then they had to leave their homes suddenly, enduring grueling marches through the desert to a place of utter desolation, where Pharaoh came close to slaughtering them. But God intervened and baptized the people in the Red Sea, bringing them into the next stage of the process by which he intended to prepare a kingdom of priests who would work with him to bring salvation to the nations. Sadly, very few survived the process. Of the 600,000 men who left Egypt, only two made it into the Promised Land. Truly the process of the Lord was neither fast nor cheap, but the result was very good.

We find ourselves in a very similar place. We have dwelt for millennia in Assyria and Babylon, praying for and contributing to the prosperity and peace of the nations where we have been exiled. We have been in these nations so long that we cannot imagine any other home. Now, before our eyes, new kings have arisen who do not know the God of our fathers, nor do they care for his people. They are leading us into ever greater oppression, removing our rights and liberties one by one even as they permit ever greater transgressions of the Commandments and created order of our God. We have prayed and prayed for salvation for our nations; we have repented for ourselves, our communities, and our leaders; we have done what we can to put away our idols and follow our God with pure hearts. And regardless what we do, matters get worse and worse. Egypt has become intolerable for us, and very soon it will become uninhabitable.

The question before us is not whether matters will get worse, but what we will do when global trials and tribulations break forth. We are entering into another season of war and upheaval such as the world has not known since the end of the Second World War. The modern order established by the First World War is now passing away, and something new is arising in its place. Will we let the waves of this upheaval wash us away, or will we cling to the Anchor which is our God and his Messiah? Will we take him at his word that he will restore his kingdom of Israel in the Land he promised to our fathers? Will we even acknowledge that we are the heirs to those promises as he has declared by his prophets and apostles?

The time has come to make this decision. Either we will rise up and claim our identity and inheritance as Israelites, or we will live out the rest of our lives in respectable mediocrity, passing from existence in the wilderness of the peoples, never to set our eyes on the Promised Land. The day of polite, but meaningless, theoretical discussion is past. The day has come for detailed plans and concrete steps. Our brethren of Judah languish, awaiting our return. Our victory is their victory; their victory is our victory. If we do not press forward to win this victory, then we will all pass from this earth, and the Name of our God will suffer great loss.

This work began with an old, familiar children's song. It ends the same way. In Christian churches around the world, children for generations have sung it:

> *Father Abraham has many sons,*
> *Many sons has Father Abraham.*
> *I am one of them, and so are you,*
> *So let's all praise the Lord!*

Do we believe this is true? If so, then let us begin to act like daughters and sons of Abraham, claiming not only the promises God made to him, but the obligations he freely incurred on our behalf.

ABOUT THE AUTHOR

Al McCarn is an avid student of the Bible who has been a disciple of Messiah Yeshua (Jesus Christ) since childhood. His world view, developed through a Christian upbringing in the American South, has shaped his thoughts and actions for his entire life. As a United States Army officer he contributed his skills and abilities to the service of his native country for nearly 30 years, including service in two wars in the Middle East and over a decade at the Defense Department in Washington, DC. Over that time he earned advanced degrees in International Relations and History, as well as professional certifications at some of America's finest military institutions. Since 2001 he and his family have been part of the Messianic and Hebrew Roots awakening that is redefining the identity of Christians through the growing understanding of their Israelite heritage. His great desire is to see the restoration of the Commonwealth of Israel under the long-expected reign of Israel's Messiah. Since 2008 he has provided commentary on the Middle East and the U.S. military to inform the prayers of intercessors connected with the Saturday morning national conference call hosted by Prayer Surge NOW. After retiring from the Army 2012 he has continued to labor in various ministry opportunities and to spread the vision of a unified Israel wherein Jewish and Ephraimite (non-Jewish) Israelites join together in anticipation of God's promised restoration of his kingdom.